HOUSE

HACKING

THE ONLY REAL ESTATE INVESTING STRATEGY
YOU NEED TO BUILD WEALTH,
LIVE FOR FREE (OR ALMOST FREE),
AND MAKE MONEY THROUGH HOMEOWNERSHIP.

BY BEN LEYBOVICH

Print & eBook design by Glory ePublishing Services

What People Say

"Let's be honest: real estate investing has changed. But inside these pages, Ben has laid out exactly what works in today's market!

I got my start house hacking, so I know the power first hand! It's about time this book was written—a guide that shows investors an inside look at this powerful strategy. And, there's no one better equipped to write it. When I need advice on a real estate deal, Ben is the first person I call. Not only can he talk the talk—he walks it every day. This book is proof. Read this book now!"

- Brandon Turner

Co-host of the BiggerPockets Podcast, author of bestseller The Book on Rental Property Investing

"Home prices have been on the rise for a decade. Using Ben's strategy, you can fight back against rising home prices so you can live where you want to live, afford a better home, or just reduce your cost of housing while enjoying extra income and appreciation.

This is not one of those real estate books touting the same old strategies that don't even work in today's market. This fresh approach is relevant today and this book explains just how to do it from start to finish.

Ben is an expert at No-Money-Down creative real estate investing. I've watched him create cash flow out of thin air. He has done it yet again with a strategy that is perfect for the new or seasoned real estate investor but is just as useful to the average aspiring homeowner."

Brian Burke

Real Estate Investor, President / CEO of Praxis Capital, Inc.

"For the longest time my go to strategy for any new investor was the method I used starting off: Purchase a duplex, live in one unit and rent out the other. It's been my solid goto recommendation to anyone that wants to get a foothold into real estate investing.

The market has become much tighter over the last few years making it harder to find a worthwhile property to do this with. Yet, there are a lot of places around the country where the vacation rental model as Ben describes it can still work very well.

I actually flew to Chandler to investigate what Ben was up to first hand. I can vouch that Ben has given a real world example of a very viable way to get into the real estate game with low risk and much higher income potential. In the book Ben covers the specifics, including all of the numbers, marketing, and management. He addresses the remodel, and describes the exact process of turning units, checking in guests.

Anyone wanting to find a way to get started or create additional streams of income needs to read this very helpful book!"

- Darren Sager

Real Estate Investor, Entrepreneur, and Licensed Real Estate Agent in NJ.

"Ben Leybovich retains his title as *the thought leader* in creative real estate investing, using it as a tool to formulate his lifestyle. Starting from nothing, Ben built a multi-family investment portfolio that allowed him to live without a W2 job. That's a dream for many. But he's now taken it a step further...forget compromise. With house hacking, Ben has solved the challenge of how to live in high-end homes, desirable locations, and expensive markets. "House hacking" is a very timely addition to the real estate investing playbook, perfect for today's economy. True to form, Ben brings a ton of personality, data, research, mechanical framework, and humor to this book-- it's everything you could ask for. If you are serious about real estate investing, lifestyle design, and locational freedom, you have to read this book."

- Justin Gesso
MBA, Bestselling Author, and Real Estate
Investor - https://justingesso.com

Acknowledgements

Success is a team sport. Very seldom does anyone ever complete a huge undertaking without help. This book is no different.

My biggest fan is my wife, Patrisha. I simply wouldn't do much of what I do if it weren't for her encouragement. Thanks so much for standing by my side in all of my endeavors, Patrisha!

I have to acknowledge that two of my dear friends provided the impetus for this book. I give special thanks to Justin Gesso, who is a friend and partner in a lot of my endeavors. Justin pushed me hard to write this book, assuring me that the knowledge of house hacking as I am describing it is something that a lot of people will benefit from. Thanks, Justin!

My friend Brandon Turner's dream is to live in Hawaii. He goes there every six months, and when he returns, the only thing I hear for about 2 weeks is how much he would love to move to Hawaii permanently. I really do hope that this book serves as encouragement to him to pursue the dream. I am hopeful that this book helps many, many people, but I must admit—while writing this book it were Justin and Brandon I imagined myself talking to.

Finally, I must acknowledge Greg Helmerick for his fabulous editing. Greg, you have a gift, my friend. Here's to big things in your future!

Thank you all!

Dedication

I dedicate this book to my kids, Aaron and Isabella. What I want most for them is to learn to see the world as a place of abundant opportunity and unlimited resources. I want them to understand, however, that looking at something is not the same thing as seeing it, and that creativity drives the means of success.

I hope that when they get older, Aaron and Isabella will glean from this book that they can have anything they want!

About the Author

Ben Leybovich is a real estate investor, author, speaker, and internet entrepreneur. He was professionally trained as a classical violinist but a diagnosis of Multiple Sclerosis (MS) in college spelled the end of his dream of becoming a professional musician.

Once Mr. Leybovich realized that his medical condition was potentially prohibitive to holding a job, he began a lifelong study of personal finance, investing, marketing, and business. Through the years, he's been involved in everything including running a non-profit music school, surviving a failed vending machine venture, succeeding in real estate investing, writing books, and selling a course online.

Mr. Leybovich currently owns and manages a portfolio of real estate investments in Ohio and manages his website www.JustAskBenWhy.com. He is an avid blogger, with publications on platforms such as www.BiggerPockets.com and www.aol.com.

Ben enjoys listening to classical music, and road tripping with his family in their Tesla Model S, which everyone (including the kids) adores.

Mr. Leybovich resides in Arizona with his wife, Patrisha, and two children, Aaron and Isabella.

Two favorite quotes:

"The only thing worse than being blind is having sight but no vision."

~ Helen Keller

"If you hang out with chickens, you're going to cluck, and if you hang out with eagles, you're going to fly."

~ Steve Maraboli

To find out more about Ben Leybovich please feel free to visit www.JustAskBenWhy.com

Table of Contents

Foreword

Ben's writing on JustAskBenWhy.com and on BiggerPockets.com has been fascinating me since 2014. I enjoy his style, one that challenges accepted norms in a direct way and makes people question their views. Ben draws his readers in and gets them emotionally invested in the story to the point of dropping their defenses enough to soak up the knowledge he dishes out.

There are many investing books on the market today, but few are truly actionable. And of those that are, most are either too bland in the storytelling department or too basic in the subject matter. In short, authors promise dreams that are not likely to be achieved.

HOUSE HACKING: The only real estate investing strategy you need to build wealth, live for free (or almost free), and make money through homeownership is different. Ben succeeds at providing us with a totally actionable blueprint for house hacking, perhaps one of the best strategies for today's economic environment and real estate cycle. And you know it's actionable because he is actually doing it right now, as this book is being published!

Do you guys know how rare this is? So many people want to write about things they did years ago, conveniently skirting the truth that those techniques are no longer viable. This book is truly unique in that it offers truly "real-time" and actionable advice.

Whether you are a new investor or are boasting decades of experience, this book will help you minimize your monthly overhead without having to drastically change your quality of life. In fact, as Ben shows us, house hacking allows you to minimize your overhead and indeed amplify your quality of life. That, my friends, is what real estate investing is all about.

Ben asked me to write the foreword and to explain some of the concepts you will see in Chapter 7. I am a CPA and run a tax and accounting firm where we work solely with real estate investors, developers, and flippers. I service hundreds of clients across the U.S., and like Ben, I contribute frequently to the BiggerPockets.com blog and forums. Chapter 7 delves into some complicated tax topics, and Ben rightly wanted an expert to discuss the details. Allow me to clarify a few points.

Ben describes short-term rental income, such as AirBnB, being subject to self-employment taxes. Self-employment taxes are another word for FICA taxes or payroll taxes. Social Security and Medicare make up 15.3% of FICA taxes. The Social Security portion is 12.4%, and the Medicare portion is 2.9%.

If you are employed, your employer withholds and pays half of the 15.3%. You, as the employee, pay the other half. But when you are self-employed, you pay the entire 15.3% on your self-employment income. Worst of all, this tax is levied before we even factor in your marginal tax rate.

Why does this matter? After all, rental income is passive, right?

No, this is not true with short-term rental income. If your average rental period for the year is less than seven days, the income is considered BnB income and is subject to the 15.3% FICA tax. If your rental period is greater than seven days and less than thirty days, and you provide substantial services (like most short-term rental hosts), you will still be subject to the 15.3% tax. You will only avoid this tax if your average rental period is greater than 30 days.

So if your investment strategy includes being a BnB host where you will receive income from short-term rentals, should you resign to the tax code and fork up the 15.3% on each dollar you earn?

Absolutely not. The tax code is full of legal loopholes that you should explore with your CPA. In the case of avoiding the 15.3% self-employment tax, we could do a number of different things. The first option is to place the property generating short-term rental income into an S-Corporation. The second option is to create a management corporation which would siphon off the profits from the short term rental, thus avoiding the tax liability created therein.

Ben touches on the second option in Chapter 7, so that's what I'll explain. Option one can get a tad complicated, and I don't want to bore you in the foreword before you even get to the gold of this book!

If you receive short-term rental income, the net income is subject to the entire 15.3% of self-employment taxes. When you move profits into an S-Corporation, you still pay taxes on the profits, but the entire profit is no longer subject to the 15.3% self-employment tax. Instead, the profits are paid out to you in the form of wages or cash dividends (distributions), and only the wages are subject to the self-employment taxes.

As an example, if you receive $10,000 net income from your short-term rental without using an S-Corporation, you will pay $1,530 in self-employment taxes. And then, assuming you are in the 25% tax bracket, you'll pay an additional $2,500 in taxes, for a total of $4,030.

If, instead, the S-Corporation manages your short-term rental property and thus receives management fees of $10,000, you may pay $5,000 of that $10,000 in wages to yourself. You will pay self-employment tax of 15.3% only on that $5,000. This amounts to $765. And then, assuming you are in the 25% tax bracket, you'll pay an additional $2,500 in taxes, for a total of $3,265.

So in the above example, the S-Corporation saves you $765 in taxes. And the really cool thing is that you'll realize those tax savings every single year. And your savings will scale as your income scales. It's truly a great strategy for sheltering your income from taxes.

Your CPA may be able to get even more aggressive than this and shelter even more income for you. This does, however, illustrate the process.

A few more thoughts.

Don't mistake an S- and a C-Corporation. A C-Corporation does not pass profits to the owner as an S-Corporation does. An S-Corporation can leave all profits within the entity, but the owner will still pay taxes on the income. This is not so in a C-Corporation. An S-Corporation also avoids the double taxation on dividends that a C-Corporation is subject to.

Last, but not least, don't place rentals with an average rental period of greater than 30 days in an S- or C-Corporation. That will lead to a ton of headaches.

I hope you enjoy the book. Ben has filled it with golden nuggets of information. It's truly a great blueprint for house hacking in today's economy.

Brandon Hall, CPA

PART 1:
It's All About Life-Design

Introduction

The Paradigm Shift

I don't know if this kind of thing ever happens to you, but I've noticed that every so often I experience an epiphany in my thinking on a given subject: a paradigm shift, if you will, whereby through a lucky synthesis of personal reflection and external triggers, I am lead to a clarity that I had not previously known.

Recently, I had one of those events—a big one, which resulted in clarity on a whole host of issues pertaining to business, money, productivity, and success. In my life, clarity of vision always leads to action, and this time is no different. The book you are now reading is a partial outcome of this recent paradigm shift.

But before I go on (don't laugh now), it so happens that I experience most of these epiphanies while in the shower. I don't think this makes me a weirdo (at least this is what I tell myself). It's the feeling of solitude that I take comfort in most, because my family has been dutifully trained to understand that when daddy is in the shower—back off. Yes, showers are good.

The Shower That Cleared My Mind

I think it's fair to say that as I am writing this book, I am already a fairly accomplished guy. What have I accomplished? Well, to start with, my wife, Patrisha, is as beautiful as she is inspirational, and our marriage represents perhaps my greatest accomplishment. My kids, Aaron and Isabella, are bright, sensitive, and well-fed! I have some real estate cash flow and some business cash flow, and conspicuously absent within the fabric of my life is anything that remotely resembles a *job*.

I work on what I want with whomever I want. I drive a Tesla Model S (which is pretty ridiculous). I travel. I speak to large groups of people. And, I live in a very nice house in Chandler (almost for free, but more on that later).

In short, I've worked hard to achieve some sense of freedom, and I have indeed achieved some.

And yet...I want more! Can you relate?

The meaning of life for me encompasses two things: the relationships I build and maintain with the people I care about and my ability to live on my own terms. What this boils down to is that I have a mission to be in control. I like to design things to be exactly as I want them to be.

While the picture I painted above likely reads pretty good to a lot of you—and it's all true—not all things in my life are where I want them to be...yet.

4

Clarity of Perspective on My Financial Ecosystem

So, what happened to me during that shower can best be described as clarity of perspective on my financial ecosystem. As I stood there under that stream of warm water, a chain of thinking ensued which lead me to fully comprehend all aspects of what I've done to get here. I realized what has worked, what hasn't worked (and why), and what I need to do more of in order to keep achieving success.

As I stepped out of the shower that morning, I saw a total and complete image of an ecosystem in which my financial life works as intended. All of the pieces of this ecosystem fell into place, and in that moment, all of them became real to me. I realized that all I have to do now is materialize some of the missing pieces.

As you can imagine, this process warrants a wide-scoped conversation deserving of a series of books discussing all aspects, phases, and tools of the ecosystem that I see so clearly in my mind's eye, with each chapter providing you with both perspective and tools for building your own ecosystem. Or, perhaps, a series of books wouldn't be enough.

But that's for later. For now, I've decided to address just one tool/technique within the ecosystem of my entrepreneurial life design. I am talking about house hacking: a technique which allows me to live in an upscale home almost for free. When done correctly (which I'll be teaching you in this book) this technique can easily allow you to live anywhere you want—any time you want—for free, or almost for free, while building your wealth!

My #1 Major Premise (to set the scene)

That memorable day, in the shower, I had many internal conversations, and one of them went like this (THIS IS IMPORTANT):

Question: Are you rich?

Answer: No. I am doing well, but I am not rich.

Commentary: If you're not rich, you cannot afford to do whatever you want just because you want to do it. An ability to completely live on your terms is the prerogative of people who've made it; you have not made it yet.

Question: OK. But we only live once. How do I design my life to incorporate all of the things which make my heart sing if I cannot simply stroke that check?

Answer: In order to have a thing, that thing must make money.

Commentary: Since I am not rich and cannot simply indiscriminately write those checks, I must adapt the position that I can have anything I want...so long as it makes money. Put differently, I can do and touch anything I want as long as I can figure out a way to rig it so that it makes money!

And as I thought about it, I realized that this is exactly what I am already doing in my life. I thought to myself:

1. You wanted to own investment real estate, but didn't have the money, so you had other people pay for it! (As of this writing, having sold some investments prior to leaving Ohio, I still own 21 rental units).

2. You love to talk to people about the power of real estate, and you love to teach. You created www.JustAskBenWhy.com so people could pay you for some of this knowledge via the CFFU. Talk all you want as long as you get paid along the way for your time and effort in education.

3. You wanted to relocate to a nicer place and send your kids to the best school you could possibly send them to. You made it possible by having someone pay your mortgage for you (house hacking). In other words, go ahead and buy the best home you or your wife have ever lived in...just be sure to have someone else pay for it.

Call it luck, providence, or divine intervention but without clearly understanding how I was doing it, I somehow managed to rig certain aspects of my life in accordance with the principle—*do it as much as you want, as long as it makes you money!*

But now, going forward, I've put a formalized approach to life-design on paper. This will not be happening on accident any longer!

The Paradigm Shift

The question is no longer, *how can I afford it?*

You can afford anything you want as long as it makes money!

Let me say this again—this is important:

You can afford anything you want, as long as it makes money!

Thus, the real question is:

This thing that I want...how do I rig it to make me money so I can afford it?

And this applies to everything. You want to live on the beach. How can you rig it to make money? You want to travel. How can you rig it to make money? You want to talk about real estate investing all day. How can you rig it to make money? You want to swim, saw, paint, write music, write books, play volleyball, get a new sports car. How can you rig it so it makes money?

Understand—if it makes you money, you can afford it! That thing you want, the thing you'd do for free all day long but can't afford to because you have family to feed and kids to put through college, that thing which makes your heart absolutely sing—*how can you rig it so it makes money, so that you can afford it?!*

Every day I roll out of bed, pee, wash my hands, splash my face, and ask myself these two questions:

1. What do I want?
2. How can I rig it to make me money?

And then I get in the shower, and the answers come to me. :)

House Hacking Freedom

Freedom means many things to different people. The amount of money in the bank, the amount of monthly cash flow, the number of revenue streams, the level of diversification of those revenue streams, the amount of time you spend managing those revenue streams, how many of the material things you want you can have, how much time off can you afford to take: all of these, and many other things, are units by which we measure freedom. Whichever works for you, I'm good with it, even if I think differently.

But regardless of how any of us defines freedom, there is one fundamental perspective that I am sure we will all agree upon.

Ultimately, freedom is a function of being able to divorce yourself from any one physical location for any given period of time. The ultimate personification of freedom is the freedom to live wherever you want whenever you want.

Let's call this ability to be where you want when you want *Locational Freedom*. House hacking is a tool that can help you do it!

A few paragraphs above, I proposed that you can have anything you want as long as it makes you money. Well, house hacking allows you to have the house you want, in any place you want, because it turns your house into a money maker, which either fully or almost fully pays for itself and therefore makes it easily sustainable for you to be there for as long as you'd like.

How Difficult Is It?

House hacking is not particularly hard, but it does require a bit of effort in a couple of different ways. First, by positioning your house this way you are either making a play for equity or income, both of which require certain skills and effort, and I will discuss both in later chapters. Also, since in order to accomplish a house hack you will need to locate the right kind of an asset (you can't do it with just any old house), you will need to put effort into locating such an asset. They don't just lie in the middle of the road.

But, if making money with your primary home and turning it from a liability into an asset is important enough to you; if living for free or almost for free in a place that makes your heart sing is important enough to you; if facilitating the kind of freedom most people don't even dare to dream of is important enough to you; then the skills and efforts involved to house hack are all very worthwhile inconveniences. And this is all they are: inconveniences. Besides, if you think about it the right way, and do exactly as I teach you in this book, things will fall into place that much easier!

Now—I am not here to tell you that house hacking is the only tool you need. On the other hand, though, it is certainly a tool in the belt that solves a particular problem in an entrepreneur's financial life, and it does so with some style and finesse. Done right, house hacking can allow us to be highly mobile, provided other elements in our entrepreneurial ecosystem are working.

And finally, I've taught for many years that in order to be effective we must be willing to *zag when everyone is zigging*. Following the masses is rarely the most effective way to get ahead of those masses. Indeed, we have to play to our strengths and do what others cannot or will not for various reasons.

Therefore, think of the house hack technique as a happy synergy of real estate investing and personal life-design which allows you to get where you're going faster by not bowing down to the convention and by being willing to do things that others won't.

What Will You Learn in this Book?

Below is a list of the topics covered within the pages of this book. You may have to re-read things once or twice, and some of the concepts may require further research. But, everything you need to know to do what I do is here! Below is the list of topics I cover:

- What is a House Hack and How Can I Make Money With It?
- Should I Buy an Investment Property, or Should I House Hack?
- What Are the Advantages of a House Hack Over a Dedicated Investment?
- A House Hacking Case Study—How I Am Living in an Upscale Home for (Almost) Free
- Which Are Better for House Hacking: Long-Term or Vacation Rentals?
- How Do I Choose the Best Location to House Hack?
- What Kind of House Works Best for House Hacking?
- How Much Money Can I Make with Vacation Rental House Hacking?
- How Much Income Tax Will I Pay on Vacation Rental Income?
- How Do I Hedge Regulatory Risk with House Hacking
- Is a 1-bedroom or a 4-bedroom Better for a Vacation Rental?

11

- How Do I Rehab my Vacation Rental House Hack for the Most Profit?
- How Do I Outfit a Vacation Rental for the Most Profit?
- How Do I Market my Vacation Rental for the Most Profit?
- How Do I Turn a Vacation Rental Between Guests?
- What Do You Need to Provide for Vacation Rentals?
- How Much Time Does it Take to Run a Vacation Rental House Hack?
- Is AirBnB, or HomeAway, or VRBO Better for Vacation-Rental House Hacking?
- Can House Hacking Pay for my Primary Home Mortgage?
- What Are Economic Losses?
- How Does Pricing Impact Economic Losses?
- How do I Know a Good City to House Hack in?
- How do I Find the Right Neighborhood to House Hack in?
- How do I Handle Safety when House Hacking?
- How do I Handle Privacy when House Hacking?
- How Much Work is it to Rent Part of my Primary House?
- Will my Mortgage Allow me to Rent Out Part of my Property?
- What Taxes do I Have to Pay with House Hacking?
- What are the Regulations on House Hacking?
- How do I Set Prices on AirBnB and Other Sites?
- And much more...

Who Is This Book For?

We bought our house hack in December of 2016. About two months later I had a conversation with my friend, who told me that he and his wife were thinking about relocating to be closer to their aging parents.

Justin left corporate employment a few years ago to go it alone, and hasn't looked back. So, the notion of losing some of the revenue sources in the move, and having to develop new ones in the new location is not too much of a concern for him. Justin knows that while it may take some time, eventually he will plug the holes, and then some.

What Justin and his wife are concerned about, though, is the fact that this new place they are looking to relocate to is quite pricey, and since there may be some hiccups on the income side of their financial equation, they are concerned about taking on the extra debt, and have been putting things off.

However, having seen me go through this house hack, and having heard all of the step-by-step in real time, Justin told me that day: *"My wife and I talked, and we've decided to do exactly what you are doing. Being able to offset the carrying costs pacifies our concerns with the temporary loss of income."*

Justin continued: *"You should write a book, Ben. You've discovered a method of dealing with the most disconcerting part of relocating—the cost of living. Knowing that there is a way to address this makes the decision to move so much easier, and it opens the possibility to so much freedom. You should write a book!"*

Another friend of mine just spent a month in Hawaii. His name is Brandon Turner, and this was not his first time in Hawaii. I think he must have taken his family there twice per year for the past three years, if not more.

The thing is, every time he comes back he says the same thing: *I wanna move there so bad!*

So—this book is for Justin and his family, Brandon and his family, and all of the folks whose heart is calling them to be somewhere but the fear of increased living expenses associated with the move is prohibiting action. Hopefully, the rationale and some of the tools I discuss in this book help you to navigate the process successfully and with confidence!

This book is also for those of you who live in some of the more expensive markets, where property costs so much that you've resigned yourself to being a tenant forever. Take a look at this article on bloomberg.com:
https://www.bloomberg.com/news/articles/2016-07-28/homeownership-rate-in-the-u-s-tumbles-to-the-lowest-since-1965

According to the latest Census data homeownership rates in 2017 plunged to the lowest level since 1965. Folks are choosing to rent in lieu of buying homes. Why? The main culprit is affordability due to home prices having outpaced growth of incomes by a good margin.

Here's the problem—rents are very much on the rise nationwide as well. So, those people who think that simply renting forever solves the problem of housing affordability are sure to be disappointed. A more sustainable solution is needed, and we have one—house hacking.

If you are willing to follow in my footsteps, and put into practice the concepts in this book, home ownership is easily achievable for you, even in the most costly markets!

Finally, as I will prove to you with hard numbers in Chapter 6, house hacking is the best way to become real estate investors for a lot of you. The cash flow I am generating with this house hack is quite simply the best and easiest cash flow of any deal I've ever done. So, if you've always wanted to be a real estate investor, but have not been able to figure out how to get your foot in the door, this book is for you.

And now buckle your seatbelts, ladies and gents. If you want freedom and passive cash flow, I'm about to tell you how!

How to Get the Most Out of this Book

I packed a lot of content into this book. I need you to understand that my main thrust here is to get you to think in the right direction. I've provided detailed numbers as they relate to my house hack, but any notion that your numbers, in your market would be same as mine is just silly. So—pay attention to the numbers but only conceptually.

Don't get stuck trying to understand how every number in this book can materialize in your market dollar for dollar as I described. The rationale is where the magic lives. It's in the perspective. It's how we look at things and what we see when we do look.

As Helen Keller put it: *"The only thing worse than being blind is having sight but no vision."*

We are talking about vision. We are talking about being able to see that which others cannot or will not. In short, my efforts in this book add up to one thing—giving you some perspective on how an abundant life is indeed within your grasp and the house hack is a tool that can help.

15

Having said this, however, because a house hack is simply a blend of that which is a home for you and your family with that which is a real estate investment, an intelligent conversation on the subject requires covering some complex real estate investing concepts. I tried to keep it light on the jargon and explained as much as possible within the confines of a book that is not meant as a real estate investing book.

I know you'll need more information to fully grasp all of the dynamics. I've prepared a few helpful tools for you. Simply follow the link below to access these.

The Book Guide

The Book Guide is a short document outlining the main concepts discussed in each chapter. As you are going through the book, the guide will help orient your thinking.

Understanding Market Values

In order to be successful at house hacking, you must be adept at estimating values of both single family and multifamily real estate. This is crucial to underwriting your exit. In the context of this conversation, it becomes crucial to understand that the methodology and technique of estimating market value in the single-family market is totally different from multifamily.

Below is a link to the Understanding Market Values eBook, in which I further explain and clarify both processes. This should be very helpful!

You can find both of these here:
www.JustAskBenWhy.com/househack

Cash Flow Freedom University

Just like the English language is made up of sentences, words, and letters, the language of real estate is made up of concepts, formulas, and numbers. I tried to give you an overview of the most pertinent terminology and numbers in this book. However, if you are truly interested in educating yourself on the finer points of real estate investing, please take a look at my Cash Flow Freedom University.

For more information please visit:

www.JustAskBenWhy.com

Chapter 1

What is House Hacking and How Can I Make Money With It?

Remember, you can afford anything you want as long as it makes money!

This is the main concept I want you to keep in mind while you read all that follows. Understand that by its very nature, if the thing you want is able to make you money, then you can afford having it, doing it, being in it, etc.

Therefore, the question before us should never be: *how can I afford it?*

Instead, the correct question is: How can I rig this thing so it makes me money, allowing me to afford it?!

So, as you get up each day, your frame of mind should be to ask yourself these two questions:

1. What do I want?
2. How can I rig it to make me money so I can afford it?

This is really very simple. Don't you agree? And past this, one additional thought to ponder is that the one criteria that constitutes freedom more so than any other is the freedom to divorce yourself from any one physical location—the freedom to choose to live anywhere you want, anytime you want, for whatever reason you want. Most people don't dare to dream of so much freedom. There is never a shortage of excuses. But don't you agree that this ability to pick up your stuff and go wherever your soul is calling you indeed personifies the ultimate freedom in life?!

Now, living in a nice place costs money (in some cases lots of money), and I am not so blinded by my own genius and exceptionally good looks that I can't see that. Indeed, cost of living is a challenge.

Therefore, if the answer to the first question (*what do I want*) is that you want to live someplace more romantic than where you currently are, then you must answer the second question as well: *How can I rig it to make money so I can afford it?*

Introducing house hacking…

What is House Hacking?

I am uncertain where the term house hacking originated. My good friend Brandon Turner, of BiggerPockets fame, likes to take credit for creating this term. Now—I don't actually know if the term is

Brandon's creation, but I figure that, if there's any possibility it is, I'll give him credit here. :)

Also, and this is a bit on a personal note, because I know that Brandon would love nothing more than to live in Hawaii full-time (although he would need to think this through as it relates to his daughter's educational opportunities), hopefully this book inspires and empowers him to take action sooner rather than later! I don't have many close friends, but Brandon Turner is definitely one.

Having said this, a house hack is essentially a blend between that which is a real estate investment and that which is a home. Basically, the thought process goes like this:

You decide you want to live someplace nice, but it costs a chunk. Obviously, unless you're independently wealthy and have the capacity to simply stroke that check, this cost is a problem. So, in order to solve this problem, you are going to think of this house as an investment instead of just a house. In other words, you will move into the house, thus making it your primary residence, but you will also rig it in such a way so that the house earns money one way or the other. This money, then, will in some way pay for enough of the cost of you being there so that being there becomes affordable, or even free.

3 Ways to Make Money with House Hacking

There are several ways you can approach this. I've never heard of anyone coming up with good titles for these methods, so I made some up:

- ❑ Equity House Hacking
- ❑ Cash Flow House Hacking
- ❑ Blended House Hacking

The premise behind all three of these methods is to offset your cost of living in that wonderful house (I often reference the cost of living as "your burn"), but each method aims to accomplish this in different ways.

Equity House Hacking

Equity House Hacking focuses on equity payoff once you sell the property, so your equity reimburses you for the cost of being there for the duration. The easiest way to conceptualize this is as a fix and flip—but with you living there for the duration of the rehab. You buy a house that needs some work because you think that after the work is done, you'll be able to sell it for much more than what you've put into it.

Here's an example. You buy a house for $225,000, and let's just say that it costs you $1750 per month to live there (via a mortgage). While living in it for a couple of years, you gradually perform $30,000 worth of repairs. You figure that these repairs will result in a sale price of $350,000.

A burn rate of $1,750 per month for 24 months means you've spent $42,000 on carrying this house. An additional $30,000 of rehab costs brings your total cash invested in the house to $72,000. Add this to the original purchase price of $225,000, and your all-in investment on this project is $297,000.

If you are indeed able to sell this house for $350,000 after two years, then you would generate a profit of $53,000 (I am not including fees here for simplicity). What this essentially means is that you live in this house at no cost for 2 years plus earn a nice and healthy $53,000 bonus for putting up with an ongoing remodel while living there.

This can work for sure, but as you can imagine, things aren't as simple as that. There are definitely issues that will arise that keep scenarios like this from being the perfect fairytale. So, I am not going to pass judgment on whether this method is better or worse than the others just yet. Keep reading.

Cash Flow House Hacking

The difference between Cash Flow House Hacking and Equity House Hacking is in the name: Cash Flow. In the equity model you don't get monthly cash flow; you won't earn anything until you sell the property. However, in the Cash Flow House Hacking model, you will instead look toward monthly income to offset your cost of living, while equity appreciation may or may not be there at the end of the day.

So what does this look like in reality? Well, I have several students who've purchased duplexes and moved into one side while renting out the other side. The rent they receive from the rental side covers all or part of their burn on the duplex. This is the classic variation of Cash Flow House Hacking.

I also have several students who are taking this model to another level by simply renting out rooms in their single family houses. This imperfect solution can represent a solution for some people because, in some markets, duplexes are hard to come by. Granted, these owners don't have children, and having a stranger in the house is not everybody's cup of tea. But, for those who want to live in places where the cost of real estate is high, this may be a worthwhile sacrifice.

Interestingly, if you read up on the current state of real estate markets, you are likely to come across articles on *"shared living."* Indeed, both rents and house prices have outpaced income growth in many of the more desirable markets, and roommates are not as uncommon today as they were even just a few years back.

More on this in a bit. For now, let me just say that while Cash Flow House Hacking is workable, this method also has some shortfalls that I'll discuss shortly.

Blended House Hacking

Blended House Hacking combines the best of both worlds, so to speak. I personally love this model because I am an ultra conservative person, and I like to hedge my bets. And, essentially, if I can win either with equity, or income, or both, I feel that one hedges the other and I'm way ahead of the game.

Here is a simplified version of the way this method works. You look for a house in an area and economy where you anticipate appreciation. Then, you buy an asset that can provide cash flow. While you're waiting for the appreciation to take hold, you are also managing to generate rental income, which offsets your burn. And if the deal also incorporates a value-add component, it makes even more sense. More on that in the next section.

Which Method of House Hacking is Right for You?

We have to acknowledge that, first and foremost, the method that's right for you is driven by the marketplace. Our minds are powerful, but we cannot outsmart the marketplace. Thus, once you decide where you want to live, you need to study the market to understand which method represents a more viable opportunity. You will learn what you need to look for as you keep reading this book.

Secondly, I've preached for many years that while it is absolutely crucial to grow and stretch yourself personally and professionally, it is nevertheless important to play to your strengths whenever possible. For instance, do you have the skills necessary for completing a hard core rehab? Do you know the difference between a footer and a rafter? Are you able to GC (general contract) your own project? If so, do that rehab, so long as the market lets you.

On the other hand, perhaps managing tenants is a better fit for you. Ask yourself which skill-set best supports your house hacking endeavor.

Third, we cannot forget that this is not purely an investment we are talking about here. You and your family are actually going to move into this house, this neighborhood, this school district, this city, this state. It is hard enough to shop for a residence without any concern for investment value. And it is hard enough to shop for an investment without worrying about whether or not it is right for your family. Finding something that works on both counts is plain challenging and requires patience and skill.

And finally, while your skill-set is important, so is your comfort zone. Again—stretching yourself is necessary but not if the stress of doing so is going to cause you to develop an ulcer, break out in hives, or have a stroke. There is no such thing as a risky deal, only a risky investor. A house hack will definitely require you to stretch; it will require you to do what others will not. But, know your limits!

The challenge of the house hack is that you somehow have to successfully marry and synthesize all of the above elements. It's a place you'll live—it's an investment. The market determines what type of an investment it is. Your skills and your comfort level do too... That's a lot of elements to synthesize! I am hoping to make this synthesis easier as we go through this book.

What Does This Look Like in Practice?

As I mentioned before, I come from a school of thought that I want everything I touch to make money. Thus, the value of any opportunity for me is pegged on its' income potential. Safety, for me, is a function of income and diversification of income. The more money I make from as many different sources as possible, the safer I feel.

Now, in my stupid youth, I made the mistake of focusing solely on income with total disregard for equity. That was indeed stupid and is a discussion in itself. Suffice it to say, I realize now that in order to drive my investment returns, both equity and income are necessary—I make a little money while I hold, and I make more money when I sell. You get the idea.

In a later chapter, I'll provide a complete play-by-play case-study, but I want to add a few words for now.

Chandler, Arizona in 2017 is still very much a growth market in terms of employment, population trends, and other economic drivers. For this reason, while real estate has appreciated dramatically since the days of the financial meltdown of 2008, there's a foundation in place that supports continued future growth—and I certainly want a piece of that growth.

Having said this, as I briefly alluded to earlier, while more aggressive than some, I am by nature a safety player. I want to hedge my bets just as much as the next guy. And, even though I am bullish on equity growth, I am cognizant that I do not have a crystal ball. For this reason, the house hack I chose to pursue has a strong cash-flow component. There is risk in everything, but I think that with my Blended House Hack, I am reasonably well hedged.

There is much more to this conversation, but it is best handled with specifics. I'll cover all of it in later chapters, so stay tuned! For now, simply remember this: *you can live anywhere you want, as long as it makes you money.*

Trust me—it's possible! Keep reading…

Chapter 2

Should I Buy an Investment Property, or Should I House Hack?

In the first draft of this book, chapter 2 was the case-study for my house hack. However, upon review, it became apparent to me that while timing and flow could indeed support placing the case-study in chapter 2, I'd be foregoing a lot of the perspective relative to my thought process leading up to why I ultimately did what I did.

The presumption I make with this book is that you will follow my advice and footsteps, which means that you will inevitably find yourself in the same position that I was in before I placed my bet. I was studying, internalizing, and rationalizing the market to figure out what I should do, where I should do it, when I should do it, and how I should do it. And relative to this, what's most important to me is that you are able to see the big picture.

I am not interested in whetting your appetite with platitudes, hurrays, and cheap theatrics. I am not interested in selling you on how easy stuff is or how quickly it can be done. There are gurus for that, of which I am not one.

While I certainly do want to entertain you, it's more important to me that you actually learn something on every page you read. What I want, and what gives me the most pleasure, is teaching. The best way I know to do this is by retracing my own steps out loud for you. I want to share my thinking with you and how it eventually materialized into my actions.

With this in mind, we need to discuss one more point before we dive in headfirst into the case-study.

When we first moved to Arizona in August of 2016 and I started looking around and evaluating my options, the very first question I asked myself was—*Should I Buy an investment property first and use the cash flow to bridge the debt service on a primary residence, or should I house hack and essentially combine my primary residence and investment into one transaction?*

I don't think this was an unreasonable question. I am a real estate investor, and these are the terms in which I think. Real estate cash flow, in one way or another, is simply there to help subsidize my lifestyle. How this happens is beside the point. I'll take what the market gives me. But, the point is, I am open to being in sync with the marketplace, and you should be too!

Both of these approaches—buying a dedicated investment property to pay for the primary, and/or house hacking—could work to accomplish, under the right set of circumstances, the stated objective of underwriting my living expenses. So, my choice was valid and reasonable. And, since at some point you might find yourself at the same crossroads, it may be helpful for you to know that in the end, I settled on a house hack as a much more elegant solution for my family.

Below are some of my considerations.

Conforming Residential Loans

In America, there are mortgage loan products which are designated for owner-occupants and those that are strictly for dedicated investment properties. I don't want this to turn into a lesson on the secondary market, Fannie Mae, or Freddie Mac, but in terms of down-payment requirements, interest rates, origination and other fees, and potentially also amortization, owner-occupied loans win out considerably.

Now, before you email me to inform me that Fannie Mae allows up to 10 mortgages (or whatever it is at the time you read this) of the owner-occupied variety for investment properties, understand that the terms on those mortgages as well as the qualifying guidelines are quite a bit more stringent than on a loan for a house that you will actually occupy.

In the end, it is always advantageous to buy as a homeowner who intends to occupy the property. This will simply and unequivocally land you the best possible terms on a loan. Once you've played this card, it's then a good idea to utilize Fannie Mae and Freddie Mac notes for as many investment properties as you can. And only once you've maxed those lines do you want to move into the commercial space.

Let's get back on point and discuss some of the particulars of how all of this knowledge shaped my eventual decision to house hack right out of the gate.

Amortization

This may not necessarily impact you in the same way as it impacts me, so have an open mind. In 2016, if I were to pursue a dedicated investment property—which is to say a piece of real estate that I intend to use for commercial purposes only without the intention to occupy it—a 30-year amortized mortgage was not achievable for me. As I alluded to above, the secondary market places restrictions on how many conforming notes used to finance a residential investment property an individual is allowed to have on his/her credit history. I've got too many, and that rules me out. I have not been able to get one of those notes for an investment property in many years, which means that whenever I buy anything other than a primary residence, I have to utilize commercial or portfolio financing.

Here's the thing: while 25-year and 30-year amortizations are not unheard of in the commercial space, the most prevalent are either 15 or 20 years. Indeed, all such loans currently in my portfolio are on a 20-year amortization.

ARMs

Aside from the obvious reality that shorter amortization periods result in higher monthly debt service, which is not the greatest thing when you're trying to create as much monthly cash flow as possible, there are other "inconvenient" commercial-paper elements as well. For instance, more often than not commercial financing incorporates ARMs and/or balloons. For those of you who don't know this yet, ARM stands for

Adjustable Rate Mortgage. With ARMs, the interest rate you pay on the outstanding balance of the note adjusts at specified times throughout the life of said note, and the rate is generally tied to some bond-rate metric.

So, payments on ARMs might start out at a 5% per annum rate and a 20-year amortization. But after, say, 5 years, the interest rate adjusts to whatever the going rate is at that time. The new monthly debt service is calculated based on the new interest rate, the outstanding balance on the note, and the remaining amortization period.

And the reason this is kind of a big deal, of course, is the interest-rate risk. In August of 2016, my thinking was that chances are better than not that the rates will be going up. Thus it is my preference, if it at all possible, to avoid exposure to potential rate hikes. In my mind, this was a strike against going with a commercial-financing plan.

Balloons

A balloon is a stipulation in the note that, after a certain period of time (but before the amortization fully reaches zero), the loan must be repaid in full. To accomplish full payoff, one can either sell the property to pay off the remaining balance organically or refinance.

So, you might start out with a 20-year loan, and your interest rate might reset in year 5, at which time your monthly debt service will adjust. This is the ARM component of your loan. Further, instead of repeating the same process at year 10, there might be a balloon stipulation instead, requiring you to completely pay off whatever balance is left on the note. This, as you can imagine, represents some risk. Why? Because the decision to sell is not a choice in this case but a mandate. What if the markets do not cooperate? Obviously, this creates a potentially dangerous situation.

What I just described is very common and characteristic of commercial-portfolio loans. In other words, there are lots of moving parts, and while you certainly have to get used to these complexities if you want to grow as a real estate investor, it's probably best to max out other options (if you have them) before considering a balloon.

Here's the thing—I had other options. The only reason I considered this route was to use the cash flow from a rental I'd be buying to cover the debt service on my primary. But the exposure to interest-rate, ARM, and balloon risks was not welcome under the circumstances. While there aren't many times in life when we are afforded clear options, I actually had options this time, so I was determined to pick the best one.

As an owner-occupant performing a house hack, I had the option of obtaining a conforming 30-year amortized note, with no ARMs, balloons, or any other junk. All things being equal, this made the option of a house hack (any type of a house hack) much more interesting to me than buying an investment property to bridge the debt service on a primary. The fact that I could achieve my equity and cash-flow objectives while not having to deal with commercial financing made a house hack a much more attractive avenue to pursue.

Does this sound complicated, or are you following along? I hope you're following, because there were more considerations that came into play. Stay with me.

Down-payments

The down-payment requirements of owner-occupied notes offer their own advantages. In August of 2016, I could qualify for a residential loan with down-payment requirement as low as 5%. By contrast, investment-property financing required a down-payment of 25%.

Those of you who know me well are aware that my preference is always for little or no-money-down financing. Putting money down equates to buying value, and I don't get excited about that. There are times when larger down payments are appropriate, specifically when you've succeeded at accumulating wealth and the game becomes more about preserving the money you've already made. But while we are in the process of building wealth as opposed to preserving wealth, we never want to buy value   we want to create it out of thin air.

That said, putting down 5% instead of 25% is appealing because I am building wealth. I presume that you are reading this book for the same reason, so let's think this through.

Two Choices

Let's say you have $50,000 to play with. The way I see it, you have 2 choices:

<u>Choice 1</u>

You could make a 25% down payment, in which case you can afford to buy a $250,000 house at 75% LTV (loan to value):

House Value = Down-payment $$$ / Down-payment % = $50,000 / 25% = $250,000

If you choose this option, the entire $50,000 will be committed to the down payment.

<u>Choice 2</u>

You could make a 5% down payment, in which case you can buy a much more expensive house. Let's say you find a house for $355,000 and make an $18,000 down payment.

There are a few points to discuss here:

One—if you go with the second option, you obviously have money left over. If you have $50,000 but the down-payment requirement is only $18,000, you have a surplus of $32,000 in your pocket. We all know cash is king, and having it is always better than not having it.

But more importantly, could you use that $32,000 to make repairs to the house, which in turn would increase the value of the house from $355,000 to, say, $425,000? If you buy the right house, the answer is yes.

Finally, if you buy a house in an appreciating market, the same percentage level of appreciation will result in more dollars considering you are starting with more value. For example, 10% appreciation on a $250,000 property would give you an additional $25,000 of value. However, the same 10% of appreciation on a $355,000 property would result in $35,500 of value. Which is better?

All things considered, the fact that I could get more house for less out-of-pocket cash by going with a residential note weighed heavily on my decision making. On all of my investment acquisitions, even those that are financed with commercial notes and require large down payments, I've always subsidized the down payment so it requires little to no out-of-pocket cash from me. But this strategy always requires complex blended-financing packaging, investors, and all the rest of the tricks I discuss in <u>CFFU</u>. The house hack strategy makes low money down as simple as possible, which makes house hacking very attractive indeed.

And thus it was becoming clearer to me that from a financing point of view, I'd be able to maximize my investment dramatically if I were willing to enter into it as an owner-occupant rather than an investor. With the amortization advantage, which would help the cash flow, and the down-payment advantages, which would not only help my reserves but maximize the rate of return, the house hack approach was starting to gain some sense of inevitability in my mind.

Interest Rates

Seven days per week (and twice on Sunday) I can get lower interest rates on an owner-occupied note than a commercial note. Interest rates put a serious dent in buying power. So, the better the interest rate I can get, the happier I am. Done—nothing much more to add here.

Management

Any way you slice it, whether this was to be a pure investment purchase or a house hack of any sort, I was going to have to manage it. I was going to have to create systems, form relationships, and in short, build infrastructure.

All things being equal, the question was—*How do I get the intended result with the least possible time investment?* Having thought about it at length, and having discussed it with Patrisha, we concluded that a well-executed, Blended House Hack was the best way to go.

Being in the same physical location as the project is simply a necessity. Granted, it is not scalable, but we weren't looking for scale just yet...only a house hack to get us planted in the new location for free, or almost free.

Easy, right? Well, not so much. Because we are very experienced landlords who have seen people behave as people behave, we knew that a poorly done blended house hack could end up accomplishing just the opposite of what we came to Arizona for. We were here to simplify and up-scale our family's life, and we were both cognizant that a poorly chosen house hack could instead compress our living arrangements and create more headaches than it was worth.

But, at the end of the day, the upside of a well-executed house hack seemed to outweigh the risk. We simply needed to be extra careful about the location and the asset itself, which would hopefully allow us to benefit from the market's upward trend. The location we chose would also help us attract guests who would be easy to manage.

All that being said, given the right location and asset, a blended house hack looked good from the management standpoint.

The Other Options

The Blended House Hack option seemed inevitable, but since I am letting you in on all of my thinking, I should mention the other two options available to me when I arrived in Arizona. Simply because we did consider them and you may as well.

<u>Continue Renting</u>

When we first moved to Chandler, we rented a nice apartment in an upscale community. We could have continued renting, but there were a few issues worth discussing that made this an undesirable option for us.

First, let me say that I think renting is an appropriate decision at some junctures in life. Renting can provide a person unparalleled locational freedom. Unlike homeownership, which for most people requires selling the home in order to relocate, renting comes with a quick and easy exit. This ultimate freedom, however, is expensive.

We were paying $1,250 per month for a 2 bedroom, 2 bath apartment on the second floor of a three story complex. Yes, this was a Class A community, perfectly located and with every amenity you can imagine. But, we were essentially paying $1 per square foot for our 1,200 square feet of space. Did I mention it was on the second floor? With no elevator?

Anyhow, for what it was, I actually think this was fair. However, neither Patrisha nor I felt like we had earned the right to pay that much for anything that wasn't making us money.

I'll say it again: I do not think that renting necessarily equates to throwing money away. I think that renting an upscale unit is akin to buying locational freedom, and in style to boot. Some day, when I've earned the right to do so, perhaps this is exactly what I'll be doing. In August of 2016, however, I simply did not feel that I'd earned that much freedom, which was one reason we were not going to continue to rent.

Another reason was that both Patrisha and I felt that we simply could live cheaper, in a much bigger place, with much better finishes, and in an equally nice location, by choosing the right house hack. As it turned out, we were right. We are now living for about 50% of what we were paying for rent.

And finally, I was then and still am now, bullish on organic appreciation in Chandler for years to come, and I wanted a piece of it. The easiest and quickest way to get in was not to rent, and not to buy a rental, but rather to house hack.

<u>Buy a Cheap House</u>

I want to tell you about one final option I considered in lieu of a house hack, which was simply to buy a lesser, inexpensive house. Everyone has a dollar amount that is a "throw-away," meaning that it is so little relative to their life that there's no sense worrying about it. If it works, just do it.

In terms of buying a house, $150,000 financed on a 30-year mortgage is that "throw-away" for me. If all it took to be where I wanted was a $150,000 house with a monthly PITI of $1,000, I probably would have just bought the house and not worried about house hacking or anything else. PITI of $1,000 per month just doesn't move my needle enough to exert creative energy to do something different. Incidentally, the reason Patrisha and I work as hard as we do is to ensure that in the future we can feel the same way about $10,000 as we do now about $1,000.

The problem in August of 2016 was that, in Chandler, a $150,000 house which cost $1,000 per month of PITI would have required us to compromise on everything, including the age of the home, the size, the amenities, the location relative to kids' school, the infrastructure—everything. Well, we weren't going to cramp our style like that, period. It wasn't what we came for. If we wanted that, we could have stayed in Ohio.

We realized fairly quickly that there was nothing interesting for us under $300,000. It appeared that a $350,000 or higher home was the solution in order for us to be in a location we wanted with the quality of construction I was seeking. The going price per square foot in locations we were attracted to was no less than $140, and more like $150 or more. Therefore, we were talking about $375,000 or more for a 2,500 square foot house.

To give you some perspective on this, I had just moved from the depressed Midwest, where I sold my house for $111 per square foot. The house was in a tiny town most people have never heard of. Had I decided to relocate to a larger city in the Midwest, such as Columbus, I would have had to spend $150 per square foot for the same type of a house.

With this in mind, I felt that pricing in Chandler, though not discounted, represented intrinsic value compared to the rest of the country. But, even if I felt that pricing was fair, this did not solve my problem, which was what?

In Lima, Ohio I was paying $1,350 PITI in order to live in a small but well-built 2006 home. Too bad it was in the middle of...well...nowhere, unless you judge quality of life by having a cornfield nearby. However, upon leaving Lima, I'd challenged myself to try and match my cost of living. This was my problem—I was challenged with matching my burn to what I had in Lima, but at the same time dramatically scaling location and asset class.

Some said it could not be done. Indeed, I doubted that momentarily too. The concept goes against the well-known proverb; *you get what you pay for.*

Now, property taxes in Arizona are a fraction of what they are in Ohio. This meant that relative to monthly cost of ownership, I could spend a bit more on the house in Arizona and still keep my monthly burn somewhat leveled. But, going from a $175,000 house in Lima to $350,000 house in Chandler did not exactly qualify as "a bit more."

As I mentioned, to be in the location we wanted and in a home which represented enough of an improvement over what we had in Lima, I would have to play in the $350,000 or higher price point. This meant my PITI would be in the neighborhood of $2,000 or more per month. That's definitely more than the $1,350 that I was paying in Lima. It was clear that some amount of delta was going to need to be subsidized, which brings us back to the house hack. I needed income to offset the higher burn!

Conclusion

While we did not discuss specific mechanics of a Blended House Hack in this chapter, I would like to think that there was some value in walking you through my thinking behind arriving at house hacking as a solution to my problem. The questions I asked and subsequently answered are the same questions you will likely ask yourself at some point should you attempt to pursue a house hack of your own. So, hopefully there was something here that you found valuable.

For us, Patrisha and I decided that the Blended House Hack model was the right avenue to pursue. Just to remind you, as it relates to house hacking, you can aim for equity, income, or both.

We wanted both!

Needless to say, the validity of my thinking hinged on being able to locate the right kind of asset, in the right location, which would allow for both income, forced appreciation, and the likelihood of organic appreciation. In the following chapters, we will dig into what that looks like in reality.

Chapter 3

A House Hacking Case Study—How I Am Living in an Upscale Home for (Almost) Free

Introduction

My wife, Patrisha, has many hobbies, one of which is telling me on a daily basis that I see everything too black and white. I mean, every household has a most commonly used phrase, and in my house its *"Ben, you see everything too black and white!"*

What can I say—some things just are black and white, don't you think? Like don't cheat on your spouse—that's rather black and white. And, real estate cycles happen and the only question is how soon and how low. Or (this is my favorite) my wife is always right—some things *are* just black and white!

Well, for me, there is another thing that's kind of black and white. It can best be expressed with the following syllogism:

Major Premise: *You live once, and you should try to do things that make you happy.*

Minor Premise: *Living in a place that makes your heart sing will help make you happy.*

Conclusion: *You should live in a place that makes your heart sing (because life's too short not to)!*

I know what you're thinking:

That's nice and lofty there, Benny-boy, so thank you for that. But, any place that would make my heart sing is liable to be pretty freaking expensive…(sigh…). Got any ideas there, Ben?!

Yes! Here's another syllogism:

Major Premise: *You should live in a place that makes your heart sing!*

Minor Premise: *You can afford anything as long as it makes you money.*

Conclusion: *You can afford a place that makes your heart sing, as long as it makes you money!*

Here we go…

Why We Did Not Choose an Equity House Hack

Just to remind you, in house hacking there are three models one could pursue:

- ❏ Equity
- ❏ Cash flow
- ❏ Blended

An Equity House Hack is an appreciation play, whereby the appreciation can either be forced through strategic value-add remodeling, organic due to market forces, or a combination of both.

In this model, you move into the house, thereby making it your primary residence for at least some time (ideally 2 years due to capital gains tax), and while there, you would perform whatever value-add you deem necessary. Think of this as basically a fix and flip, but with you living in the house. And hopefully, while you are there, the market cooperates with some organic price inflation as well.

This model works well with high-end properties for several reasons. First of all, labor and materials for a $1,000,000 house cost more than those for $250,000 house, but not linearly more. This means that the delta is much better in high-end house hacks.

Additionally, as I mentioned in the previous chapter, if we assume organic appreciation, the larger valuation gets you more money through price inflation. In other words, 10% appreciation on a $250,000 house gets you $25,000 of value. But, the same 10% appreciation on a $1,000,000 house gets you $100,000 in value. If you have a choice, which would you choose?

After 2 years of living in this house, the capital gain you receive on the sale is free from taxation—might as well go big and pay no taxes.

Those are some of the advantages of higher-priced equity house hacks. There is, however, a significant problem with this model—the carrying costs.

To carry a $1,000,000 house for 2 years is not what you would call a cheap endeavor, and since there is no income to offset the burn, there is a rather heightened risk profile. If something happens and you are not able to exit on the timetable you planned or at the delta you thought, you'd be, as they say, screwed, having to now carry this thing indefinitely, in which case I really hope you like the house.

This, my friends, was enough to deter me.

Why We Did Not Choose a Cash-Flow House Hack

Unlike the Equity House Hack, which places 100% of the money-making emphasis on equity, a Cash Flow House Hack is focused solely on income. While the former is akin to a fix and flip but with you living in the house for the duration, the latter is basically a straight cash-flow rental.

The basic objective is to find a dwelling which, in terms of the layout, lends itself in one way or another to leasing a portion of the space. If you don't mind someone actually living in your home with you, this could be as easy as buying a house with more bedrooms than you need and renting out the spare bedroom. Or, this can be a duplex, triplex, or fourplex, with you living in one of the units and renting out the rest. The bottom line in this strategy is that the resulting rental income subsidizes your carrying costs on the asset, which makes it affordable for you.

Unlike an Equity House Hack where the only profit model is to create equity which you realize on the sale, a Cash Flow House Hack involves someone (your renters) essentially subsidizing your burn for you, so the profit model is debt pay-down.

While there is potentially more profit in the equity model, there is also a lot more risk because it is so reliant on market valuation (as is any flip). By contrast, while a Cash Flow House Hack is a lot slower at generating wealth on your balance sheet, it is a lot safer and offers a ton of financial relief due to the fact that someone else is carrying the home for you, which means you can hold onto it indefinitely, and this means you never have to be forced into selling unless it is on your terms.

In the end, however, I chose not to pursue the pure cash flow model either. Being that I am an investor, I am keenly aware that appreciation on the back-end is very much needed to drive investment returns, especially as it relates to the IRR. Yes, my primary objective was to subsidize my monthly burn. However, I wanted to make money on this thing, and for that I needed equity appreciation, which a pure cash-flow play didn't offer.

It just so happened that, in 2015 and 2016, Maricopa County, Arizona was the fastest growing county in America. Chandler (specifically South Chandler) with all of its employment base is still in big-time growth mode in 2017. I was bullish on it, and I wanted exposure to it.

I knew that, given the right kind of house, the chances of organic price inflation were better than 50/50. Additionally, if I were to find a deal which also incorporated some elements of forced appreciation, I would really have a winner.

But at the end of the day, while I'm bullish on equity, I am not in possession of a crystal ball, and thus I wanted to hedge my bets.

I did not want to ask: *Will I win?*

I asked instead: Which way will I win first?!

The answer was in combining income and equity!

We Chose to Pursue a Blended House Hack!

It's the best of both worlds. On one hand, the income would subsidize all or part of the holding costs, which diminishes our risk profile in the event market valuations tanked. On the other hand, because our holding costs would be subsidized, we could opt for a much more expensive house, which would (at least in theory) be more desirable and therefore more likely to be subject to organic price inflation if the market trends held.

And a nice side-effect is that living in a home like this is inherently more fun. We came to Arizona looking for more fun, so this worked just fine!

Financial Criteria

Let me begin by saying that I really did not want to spend any more than $50,000 - $60,000 in cash on this project. Furthermore, since I was looking for value-add, I figured that about $20,000 - $30,000 would necessarily be invested into the rehab, leaving me with about $30,000 to cover the down-payment and closing costs. This meant that the lower the down-payment the better.

Well, 5% down-payment on a $300,000 house is $15,000, and on a $500,000 house it is $25,000. I could make either on the right project. And, I was able to qualify for both notes, so that wasn't a factor.

What mattered more to me, and what was the most crucial financial element, was the juxtaposition of the potential income on this house hack to the PITI burn. Yes, I wanted appreciation, but what I wanted first and foremost was the freedom and safety which comes with subsidizing my burn.

Here are some thoughts that were running through my head at that time:

The Math

As I mentioned earlier, my house in Ohio cost me about $1,350 per month, and when we left Ohio, I made it a personal objective (and challenge) to try to position our cost of living in Arizona to be equivalent to or better than what we had in Ohio. What made this challenging was that I also wanted to up-scale our quality of life, which was why we left Ohio in the first place. I wanted a much nicer, bigger house in an infinitely better location, but I wanted all this for the same burn, or less...hahaha (on the second read-through this sounds hilarious, but it was true!).

In mathematical terms, what I wanted was for my new PITI burn, after the house hacking income, to be $1,350 per month or less.

51

Here's how I approached this. The income was the known factor. If I was going to buy a duplex in XYZ location, for example, I would know what the income was going to be. This is not hard. It's called market research. And from here, all I needed to do was to subtract the income from the proposed PITI and arrive at a figure equal to or less than $1,350.

For example, if I thought that my rental income would be $800 per month, the highest carrying cost I would be willing to accept for my new house was $2,150 per month. Why was this my target figure? Because my burn delta would be $1,350, which was my target:

Burn Delta = - PITI + Income = - $2,150 + $800 = - $1,350

And from there, it wasn't hard to arrive at my maximum purchase price. I knew my down-payment (5%), I could approximate the interest rate (5%), and the HOA and property taxes were, of course, known. When I walked the numbers backwards, for projected rent revenue of about $800, and maximum burn of $2,150, my maximum purchase price would have to stay around $375,000. I could spend more if I could assume more rental revenue. I would need to spend less if I predicted less rental revenue.

And, of course, all I was doing here was working to keep my burn at the same level as it was in Ohio: $1,350 per month. Naturally, if at all possible, I wanted to do better!

Duplexes Did Not Work

The first thing I searched for was a suitable duplex. Combining an investment property with a primary occupied residence for your family is a tricky proposition indeed. But, this was the most direct path I knew of.

Segue: Don't laugh, but I stopped writing for a minute to welcome a Casita guest arriving just now. Usually, I am not present for this process because everything is automated and happens in my absence, but I happened to be here writing. The gate bell rang (actually the bell is wired to ring my phone through the landline), and through the big triple window in my living room, overlooking the beautifully quaint courtyard, I saw my guest standing there at the gate—it was the first time I was actually here to greet someone in person. It was kind of cool!

This is important: I will dissect this issue later on, but, not just any house lends itself perfectly to a Blended House Hack. In my house, I have a gate and a courtyard separating the Casita from the main house. It was hard to find this house, but I am going to teach you what I looked for and what I saw, because it worked out more than perfectly. Keep reading!

PS: She will stay 4 nights, and before she checks out through VRBO, she will deposit about $271 into my account.

OK, back to why the duplex didn't work. Unfortunately, in the part of Chandler we wanted to live, there were no duplexes. And I don't mean that there weren't any for sale. What I mean is that they just didn't exist in the locations that could work for us. To continue pressing for a duplex would have meant expanding the distance to our kids' school (and drive time), and looking in areas where the age and quality of the construction were less than desirable to me.

Simply put, I did not pack up the Tesla, put the kids in it, and schlep for 5 days from Ohio to Arizona just to end up in some duplex that was a 45 minute drive from school. House hack or no house hack, we came to live it up, not down. We came to make life more beautiful and convenient...and rich! We were not prepared to cut corners. I needed a plan B.

Needing a plan B was both good and bad. It was bad because it prolonged the search and made it more difficult and frustrating. A duplex would have been the most straightforward solution to our problem. Instead, I needed to get more creative and more knowledgeable about the marketplace. The really good thing, though, was that in the end I designed a strategy which ended up being infinitely better than a simple duplex hack.

Multi-Generational Living

Where Chandler-area neighborhoods lack in small multifamily residences, they make it up with something called Multi-generational Single Family residences. The idea is simple—Arizona is where young people come to work and older people come to retire. Combine the two, and the notion of a floor plan capable of accommodating both is not so far fetched.

What this type of floor plan looks like in practice is that there is usually a main house with 3, 4, or 5 bedrooms and 2 or 3 baths. But additionally, there is a guest house, which is either attached or detached from the main house, but it typically has its own bathroom and its own entrance, making it perfect for your wife's mother (or anybody else that needs to live with you, but not *with* you).

In the Midwest, they call it the mother-in-law suite, though you hardly ever see them in the wild. In the Southwest they are called Casitas, and they are not nearly as scarce.

In the Leybovich household we have a name for it too. We call it...wait for it...*cha-ching*!

More on that later...lol.

The more I thought about this, the more I decidedly liked the idea of a house with Casita. For one thing, it was still considered a single family residence, which meant that I'd be able to finance it with a conforming note, benefitting from the lowest interest rate and down-payment requirements. Additionally, I felt that by late 2016 pricing on multifamily was starting to reach too high, while single family was not anywhere near the top. And finally, the pool of buyers for a single family house like this is infinitely larger than a duplex, which was a good thing for when I was ready to sell.

All of this meant that my exit looked less cloudy and organic price inflation was more likely. And most importantly, I could buy one of these houses in an infinitely better location than a duplex!

Therefore, all things being equal, if the Casita could generate sufficient income to offset my living expenses and get me back down to that $1,350 monthly burn that I had in Ohio, I was all in. It was clearly a better option than anything else I'd considered. Using a Casita for my house hack offered more desirable features like an upscale house, more room, easier exit, better location, and more chance of riding the appreciation train in Chandler.

We Found the House!

We made a ton of offers on a ton of houses. Some already had Casitas, while others had floorplans conducive to making one fairly easily. I looked at all options, and then we found it.

The house was listed for around $380,000. My wife had her real estate sales license by then and represented me. My first offer was $300,000. I am pretty sure I pissed some people off. I did not get a counter.

The house sat for about a month, and the ask was lowered. I came back with a higher number (can't remember what it was, to tell you the truth). In the end, we went under contract at $355,000.

We will mention certain pertinent aspects of the house as we go through this book. For now let me just mention that aside for the 3 bedrooms and 2 baths in the main house, and this 2nd floor office, the house has a Casita with its own bath, which is the central element of this book.

I figured that on a long-term lease I could realize monthly rent of $600 for this Casita—strictly because of the location. I knew that I'd have to figure out a kitchenette of some sort, and I would need to attract the right kind of tenant, but I thought I could do it.

However, as Patrisha and I considered where we lived, which was 12 minutes from Intel, PayPal, Wells Fargo, etc., and also in the middle of vacation paradise, it became increasingly clear that the vacation rental model was likely the better way to go. In Chapter 4, I will discuss a lot of the thinking behind this decision.

The Result—We are Living Almost for Free!

The PI (principal and interest) on our house hack is $1,708 per month. The property taxes are about $215 per month. Fire insurance is about $50. All in, our burn totals about $2,050 per month, plus or minus $50.

As of this writing, the Casita has been up on AirBnB and VRBO for about 3 months. During these 3 months it has generated about $4,100 of cash flow. In a later chapter, I will go through the complete underwriting of all of the numbers, and you will see that a very reasonable expectation for our average monthly cash flow is right around $1,300. Some months will be less and some much more. But on average, we should net $1,300 per month.

With this $1,300 subsidy against the PITI, our monthly burn delta should average plus or minus $750.

If this isn't sinking in for you yet, let me rephrase:

My family and I are now living in a much nicer home, in a much more economically diverse town, in beautiful and sunny Arizona where we have blue skies, palm trees, and sunshine almost every day of the year, and it's costing us half of what we paid to live in Ohio. Our quality of life has improved dramatically. We're living a bigger and better life for about half the money!

General Perspective

First—you can't get even a remotely decent apartment for $750 in Chandler. Hell, as I am writing this, I just rented a 2-bedroom 1-bath unit in Lima, Ohio for $700 per month, and this was a discounted rate because I rented to an existing tenant wanting to upgrade. I have another 2-bedroom 1-bath coming up within the month and I bet I can get $725 per month for that one. And this is in Lima, Ohio!

Second—I came to Arizona looking to improve my family's quality of life while keeping our housing burn down to $1,350 (same as Lima). I am not sure, but I think a $750 burn is better than $1,350.

And we are living in beautiful Chandler, Arizona, in a house almost twice the size, with a pool, granite, travertine, and all the rest...think about that!

Can you do it? Would you like to try? Would you like to scale your quality of life while decreasing your cost of living by 50%?!

Conclusion

The basic principles are as follows:

Major Premise: *You should live wherever makes you happy.*

Minor Premise: *You can afford anything as long as it makes you money.*

Conclusion: *You can live anywhere you want, as long as it makes you money!*

The paradigm shift for me was the realization that I can afford anything...so long as I can figure out how to make money with it.

There are many more details to discuss relative to how I run things and why things work the way that they do. In the following chapters, I will try to answer some of the most pressing of these questions.

For now, it is time for me to vacate the lounge chair by the pool that I've been occupying while writing this chapter for the last 2 hours and take the kids to the park. Maybe I forgot to mention this, but we have an amazing park 3 minutes walking distance from the house. Since the weather is so great here, we can go year round.

PART 2:
It's All About the Numbers

Chapter 4

Which Are Better for House Hacking: Long-term or Vacation Rentals?

I would hope it's quite apparent by now that what I am attempting to do in this book is to answer your questions before you ask them. These are the very same questions I had to work through as I was considering my own options, and so I hope you find the answers useful.

That said, one of the most pertinent questions is this:

Which Are Better for a House Hack: Long-term or Vacation Rentals?

There is one absolute here that needs to be underscored to begin this conversation, and it is this:

It's all about the market, stupid!

ιle there are pros and cons to both/either, the fact is that the ιarket, more so than anything else, dictates which type of rental is more appropriate for you to pursue. With a rental, just as with any other product, you are bringing a product to the marketplace which fulfills a need. So—which is a more acute need that will allow you to achieve your objectives faster? Study your market to find the answer.

The other way to look at this is to acknowledge that, in some ways, your decision to relocate to a specific market has to be driven by the very opportunities the market presents. In other words, if you decide that you really want to focus on vacation rentals as part of your house hack, then moving to a market which doesn't support the vacation rental model is kind of silly. Make sense?

It's a Matrix

Realizing that holding a rental of any type will require some effort and that it will indeed constitute some amount of risk, what we are doing here is trying to synergize and balance 3 elements:

- ❏ Risk Exposure
- ❏ Necessary Effort
- ❏ Profit Potential

There is a golden mean in there somewhere whereby, for the lowest amount of effort and lowest level of risk, we are able to make the most money.

Think of it this way. If you had to choose between an opportunity to earn $300,000 per year which required you to work 80 hours per week and travel non-stop, or $120,000 per year while working about 10 hours per month, which would you choose? Would you take less money for much less time commitment, or would you trade your time for more money? Or, if you don't consent to working 80 hours per week for $300,000, is there an amount that you would do it for? How about $500,000? A cool million? What is the golden mean in your personal equation?

Here is another example. Say you had an opportunity to participate in an investment which could generate a $500,000 return within 24 months but requires a personal guarantee from you, meaning it requires you to sign personal recourse whereby you could lose your house, cars, etc—would you do it? Would you take on this much risk for a potential payoff of $500,000 within two years? No? Okay, then. How about for $1,000,000? Or, would you instead take an investment that could yield $125,000 within the same time-frame, but does not require a personal guarantee and is therefore a lot less risky? What is your personal golden mean for this equation?

You see, everything we do in our financial life has to synergize the benefits with time spent and risk assumed. Every enterprise has a golden mean whereby the benefits out way the risk and time commitment. The discussion around whether a long-term rental or vacation rental is better for a house hack is no different. So, let's assess the two.

Stability

This is the crux of my entire dilemma after buying my house hack. I know rentals. I've done rentals for a decade. Frankly, rentals are the most stable income I've got, and I have ten years of experience to base this on. Sure, things go sideways at times. But over the long haul, nothing beats rental income.

On the other hand, I just didn't know how well I'd do using my Casita as a vacation rental. Based on market research, I assumed that this was the better way to go, but I simply didn't have any personal prior experience to back that up.

For this reason, I must admit that all throughout the process of renovation, the notion of simply renting the Casita long-term was attractive to me. In the end, I did take a chance on going the vacation-rental route, and I am glad that I did, but using the Casita as a long-term rental was definitely something I considered.

Time Commitment

This is another area where the long-term rental situation has an advantage. After all, with vacation-rental guests coming in for 3,5,12 days at a time, the prospect of turning this Casita 4 to 6 times each month seemed over the top and somewhat intimidating.

Again, just as in the stability-of-income category, the long-term rental situation had its appeal. My thinking at this point was that in order to compensate for these deficiencies, the vacation rental model would need to generate substantially more financial gain.

Let's discuss this.

Magnitude of Income

To get us started in this conversation, allow me to paint a picture for you. I want you to think of money in your life as a river, and I'd like you to think of yourself as a mesh filter positioned within the money river. Most of the money flows around you, but some flows through you. And as money flows through you, though much of it comes out on the other side, some of it gets stuck to you. This imagery provides a couple of interesting points to note.

As good of a filter as you may be, if you are busy sunbathing on the riverbank instead of working hard inside the river, you've got no chance of catching anything, let alone serious money. This is a bit abstract, and perhaps even somewhat eccentric and esoteric, but are you getting this imagery?

You've got to be in the game in order to have a chance at winning!

Now, if we take this imagery one step further, I might be able to convince you that there are three elements directly responsible for how well your filter catches money. The first we just discussed—you've got to engage!

The second, quite predictably, has to do with how fine your filter is. In our kitchen, Patrisha has four of these mesh strainers, but you know something? Only one tends to get all of the use. Why? It's the best at catching the most particles. So, while the first element of success is just to engage, the second has to be to refine your filtering skills.

But there is one more crucial element here, and it is the river's velocity—the faster the stream, the more money you have an opportunity to catch!

Velocity of Money

Now we've arrived at a concept economists appropriately refer to as Velocity of Money (VOM). Think of VOM as the speed with which money travels throughout the economy by way of transactions at any given period of time.

It isn't difficult to see that the faster the VOM, the more transactions are taking place. And more transactions taking place is implicit in consumer confidence. And, if consumers are more confident, they spend more money, and they increase the velocity of money...and the cycle goes on.

By the way, the consumers in this case are both corporations and individuals, with the only difference being that while consumers buy mostly goods and services, while corporations also buy raw materials. The point is—when folks are more confident, they spend more money, they spend it faster, they create a higher VOM, and the economy grows healthier.

What happened in the great recession of 2008 was just the opposite—the velocity practically came to a stand-still. That's like your heartbeat coming to a standstill. Velocity is like oil flow throughout the ICE engine. If oil stops flowing, the whole thing seizes up. Not good!

Coming Back to Magnitude of Income

The thing I innately sensed when making the decision to pursue vacation rentals as part of our House Hack was that this path represented much faster VOM through more transactional activity, and therefore my Casita (which in this case is my mesh-filter) was going to be able to catch more dollars. And indeed, in the first 48 hours after going live on AirBnB and VRBO, we booked 3 stays for a total of about $800 after fees to those platforms. And before the first month was over, we'd booked $1,600 of pre-tax cash flow.

By comparison, I believe that the maximum rent I'd be able to get on a 12-month lease for this Casita is $600 per month, and only because the location is so desirable. This means that the vacation rental income-potential for the Casita is more than twice the long-term rental income.

The main concept to remember here is the Velocity of Money—kind of a big deal!

For Math Geeks and Investors

Those of you who are familiar with some fancier investment math are likely aware of something called Internal Rate of Return (IRR). For my money, this is the absolute best way to track investment returns. For one thing, the IRR time stamps cash-flow events and discounts the value of these events relative to the elapsed time. Also, the IRR calculation requires either closure of the cash flow loop with the return of capital or the projection thereof.

Most investment-return metrics that people like to use, such as the Capitalization Rate (Cap Rate), and Cash on Cash Return (CCR) are what we call *static metrics*. These are simply snapshots in time.

However, you know as well as I that because of inflation and opportunity cost, a dollar today is more valuable than at any time in the future. And if this is so, then in order to really understand—in apples-to-apples terms—what value in today's dollars tomorrow's cash flow really represents, we need to somehow account for time.

Well, long story short (because this is a house-hacking book...not an investment book) we use the IRR to do just that—take into account what future cash flows might look like, discount them relative to the time frame, and render a calculation which tells us the return of future cash flows in today's dollars. Apples to apples.

The reason I am telling you all of this is just to help you understand the importance of the Velocity of Money in yet another way. You see, receiving $1,000 today for me is worth $1,000. Why? Because I know what I can buy for $1,000 today. But receiving the same $1,000 in 3 years is worth much less to me. Why? Because I don't know how much I can do with $1,000 in 3 years. Blame inflation or uncertainty of what'll happen in the economy to cause the buying power of this currency to erode, but I prefer $1,000 today. Plus, there is the simple fact that if I had the money sooner, I could reinvest it sooner.

It's all about Velocity of Money! Earlier, I tried to describe it in somewhat liberal-arts terms. Mathematically, it all comes down to the Net Present Value of future cash flows (NPV).

Lots more can be said, but guys—this is a house-hacking book, so I need to get back on point. But, my background is in real estate investing. If this kind of cerebral perspective on numbers is something that excites you, please check out my Cash Flow Freedom University.

Conclusion

This was an interesting discussion of the synergy of time commitment, risk factors, and income potential. For some of you, long-term rentals as part of your house hack are just what the doctor ordered. They bring in less income, but the income is more predictable and requires less effort to maintain. But for the rest of you who are like me and want the most money you can get as fast as possible and are willing to put in the work to exploit the Velocity of Money, you'll want to explore vacation rental house hacks.

You can have anything you want so long as you can rig it to make you money!

Chapter 5

How Much Money Can I Make with Vacation Rental House Hacking?

Introduction

Before we dig into the specifics, I need to underscore that our primary objective with any type of house hack is to offset living expenses. Unlike a pure investment asset whereby the sole purpose is simply to make money, a house hack—specifically a Blended House Hack—is there to fulfill a very specific function. We aim to make enough income to offset increased expenses so that it becomes possible for us to live where we want to live without being financially strapped. Meanwhile, the long-term goal of holding this asset is to realize enough equity growth so that when we are done, our exit is easy and potentially lucrative. This brings me to my next point:

It's About Locational Freedom

The overarching purpose of this book is to address the issue of locational freedom. I want to teach you how to use some form of house-hacking strategy to facilitate the objective of affording to live the way you want, where you want. As entrepreneurs (and as human beings) we are constantly in search of freedom. What makes you and I different from so many other people is we are brave enough to admit to ourselves that life without freedom is garbage!

So many people out there are incapable of crossing over this intellectual-honesty threshold, and they end up spending their days telling the world how much they hate their job, house, car, and life, but telling themselves it's the best that they can do so they'd better just be happy about it.

But whether we admit it or not, freedom is what all of us want, either consciously or subconsciously. The ability to come and go as your heart and circumstances require is likely the greatest expression and personification of freedom.

That said, here's an important distinction. Coming and going as you please is a function of two elements, namely coming—and going. As we discuss freedom in terms of being able to pick up our stuff and move elsewhere, we must not lose sight of the reality that eventually we may want, or need, to leave that next place. What goes up must come down, so to speak. With this in mind:

In real estate, the exit dictates the entry 100% of the time, and it's detrimental to lose sight of that!

Relating this to house hacking, the exit is why I did not pursue an Equity House Hack whereby there was no income component. I have too much respect for the market to hitch my exit to nothing but speculation. However, in the same vein, a pure Cash Flow House Hack has similar problems.

For example, let's say you buy a house for $300,000. Let's also assume you are able to generate enough cash flow by renting out some part of the space so that you are living for free, or least very comfortably. That's great! The cash-flow aspect of this house hack is a success.

But, let's just say that tomorrow you decide it's time to move on. Now you are required to sell your house because you don't want to keep it as a rental and manage it from a distance. So you list the house with a real estate broker, but you learn that the market value of your house today is $289,000. And to make things worse, that $289,000 represents the top of the market for your house in pristine condition. But it's likely your house is not in pristine condition.

Hmm. When you bought this house, it was worth $300,000 to you. Why? Because the layout of this house provided you the opportunity to house hack. Since all of your energy was fixated on the potential income you could generate to offset your burn, you neglected to realize that while you see this house's value as a function of its cash-flow house-hacking qualities (meaning you pin this house's value on its income), the rest of the market will not necessarily see things that way!

And indeed, you may learn that, to the rest of the marketplace, yours is just another single-family residence, only now it's a few years older...and with a few more scratches (thank your kids for those). So what if there is a private entrance into one of the bedrooms? This may or may not be of any value to the marketplace.

Are you getting the picture? In short, having the "income blinders" on has prevented you from considering your exit through the eyes of your potential buyers. This is no better than having "equity blinders" on, thinking real estate will appreciate forever.

Exit, my dear friend, has nothing to do with how you see things—it's all about how other people see things. It's all about the market!

If we are going through this house-hacking exercise under the banner of locational freedom, it's not good enough to be able to come as you please; you also have to be able to leave as you please. This is where taking care of the equity appreciation becomes paramount!

OK—so that was a bit of a mouthful, but I thought it was necessary to establish some perspective on this as part of a larger conversation on how much money can be made with vacation rentals. Now that I've got your head spinning in a million different directions, allow me to make this entire equity piece very simple for you.

Focus On Vacation Rentals!

What we are talking about is a vacation rental house hack, where the operative words are *vacation rental.* Follow my logic:

If: If you are able to use a vacation rental as a tool

Then: The marketplace in which you bought your house hack can be described as a destination point

If: The marketplace in which you bought your house hack is a destination point

Then: There are some intrinsic characteristics present that are conducive to organic market strength and market growth

If: There are intrinsic characteristics present that are conducive to organic market strength and market growth

Then: Then: Not only is your cash flow likely to be strong, but you are likely to see organic price inflation over time.

Indeed, it will be difficult for you to run a viable vacation rental in middle-of-nowhere, corn field, USA, unless it's a vacation hot spot full of cows and pigs. There must be organic demand. There must be vacationers, retirement draw, corporate event destinations, employment base growth, etc.

Simply put, if your vacation rental is going to be successful, it is because there are strong intrinsic reasons for people to be in this marketplace. And, by default, if there is strong demand, there is usually price inflation!

So, the conclusion we arrive at is this:

Wherever vacation rentals will be successful, equity should appreciate over time.

House hacking in such a location, therefore, more than likely qualifies as the blended variety, at least as that applies to organic appreciation. From here, to be really safe, we can look to buy something with a bit of a value-add component, thereby solidifying our exit.

Back to How Much Money You Can Make with Vacation Rental House Hacking

The income from vacation rentals is a basically combination of two elements: nightly rate + applicable fees. I want you to stop reading now and take a few minutes to create a free account on the following platforms.

1. AirBnB.com
2. VRBO.com
3. HomeAway.com

There are many others, but these are the big boys. At the time of this writing, VRBO is owned by HomeAway. Look around and compare what's available on all of these platforms in whatever your specific desired market is. I'll compare and contrast these in a later chapter, but for now simply see what you can see.

Nightly Rates

Obviously, this is very location-specific and season-specific. Just to create a snapshot in time for you, I am looking on VRBO for available 1-bedroom units for the date range of 4/26/17 - 4/30/17.

Here's what I see:

San Diego, CA: $164/night is the least expensive. $225/night and up from there.

San Francisco Bay Area: Lots in the $120 - $500 range.

Denver, CO: $95/night is the least expensive.

Waikiki, Honolulu, HI: $120 - $220/night range.

Dominican Republic: $75 - $150/night range.

Chandler, AZ: $65/night is the least expensive (mine). Range is $70 - $120.

Miami Beach, FL: Lots in the $250 - $795 range.

This gives you a good idea of what 1-bedrooms are going for in various locations during a specific date range. Keep in mind, though, that this does not necessarily tell you what the owners are actually getting. Let me explain.

Owners are at liberty to negotiate with guests. So, a $150 per night listing may very well be renting for $115, but this information is not public. Thus, this isn't a black and white process.

Underwriting Our Casita's Income Potential

Let's do the math together. This is important as it's exactly what you will need to do for your own house hack.

Step 1: As of this writing, I advertise my Casita at $65 per night, and I do not increase my booking fee for the weekends. Thus, if I could book my Casita for 365 nights per year, it would yield a total of $23,725 of GSI (Gross Scheduled Rental Income):

$$365 \times \$65 = \$23,725$$

Step 2: The reality, however, is that booking 365 nights per year is unlikely. During vacation season, for example, the unit is occupied 25 nights out of the month, leaving 4 or 5 days between guests. Can 30 nights per month happen? Yes. Will it happen every month? No.

Furthermore, you will find that once you buy and move into your house hack, many months you will have some form of guest you don't charge to stay there for a day or two. I say this based on my own track record living in the paradise that we live in and having family and friends all over the country. They will come to visit you, and you probably won't charge them.

25 billable nights per month seems reasonable, in which case:

$$25 \text{ nights} \times 12 \text{ months} \times \$65/\text{night} = \$19,500/\text{annum}$$

So, if we could sustain bookings at a rate of 25 nights per month, and at $65 per night, we would earn an annual yield of $19,500 from the Casita.

Step 3: However, Arizona vacation rentals are cyclical. Why? Because it gets hot enough for 4 months out of the year that vacationers go elsewhere. So, we don't really expect a 25-nights-per-month booking rate during June, July, August, and September.

On the other hand, because we are only minutes from Intel and the Price Corridor, aside from vacationers we also attract business travelers. In fact, as I am writing this, our current guest is here on contract work for 4 days. She is a marketing and branding specialist and is evaluating a local coffee shop. Our next guest is coming in for their pilot license recertification at a local airstrip, which is only a hop and a skip from our house. And the guest after that is a COO who just transferred here from another part of the state and is in currently in search of permanent living arrangements.

The reason behind all of these people being here in our Casita is much less a function of anything to do with weather and more a function of a growing economy. So, while we will definitely see a drop off in vacation travelers, there will still be some booking activity during the off-season months. Let's be safe and say 10 nights out of the month for the 4 months in question.

Step 4: This means that our total projected monthly occupancy is 25 nights for 8 months, and 10 nights for 4 months, for a total projection of 240 nights:

$$(8 \times 25) + (4 \times 10) = 240 \text{ nights/year}$$

If we book all 240 of those nights, our projected booking revenue is $15,600:

$$240 \times \$65 = \$15,600/\text{year}$$

Note: we began with $23,725, but having discounted it to account for various vacancies, we now believe that our realistic booking revenue is $15,600 per year.

We Charge Fees

I will discuss this in more detail in a later chapter, but in addition to nightly booking fees, all of the platforms you'll be using to market and book your vacation rental allow owners to charge other appropriate fees. As you dig into your market analysis, however, you'll realize that while more fees are available, most owners assess only a cleaning fee, and the way free-market competition works is that if no one else charges any other fees, neither can you. If you do, you risk losing your competitiveness in the marketplace. So, all things being equal, what we are talking about is the cleaning fee.

Step 5: For our Casita, we charge a cleaning fee of $35 per booking. We do not do any cleaning whatsoever during the guest's stay, so this $35 covers the turn after the guests check out. Considering that our average stay is 5 nights, and based on a total season of 240 nights, this amounts to additional revenue of about $1,600 per year:

$$\$35 \times (240 \text{ nights} / 5 \text{ nights}) = \$1,600/annum$$

Step 6: Let's add this to the projected booking revenue and round things off to say that our Casita is capable of generating about $17,000 per year. This is what we call Effective Gross Income (EGI).

Step 7: Now, I am not sure how you function around money, but I would much rather like to be presently surprised by the upside rather than unpleasantly surprised by the downside. So, let us be really conservative and discount our EGI by 20%. If so, we can underwrite a very conservative, discounted-to-high-heavens EGI of around $13,500 per year:

$$\$17,000 \times 80\% = \$13,500 \text{ (rounded)}$$

Event Pricing

Now that we've established what we think is a conservative potential top-line revenue, let's not over-penalize our Casita. After all, our house hack happens to be about 30 minutes from the stadium where Ohio State had it handed to them by Clemson in a 2016 bowl. We just missed bringing our Casita on-line for that event, but the nightly rates during events like this increase by as much as 100%.

Arizona, due its pleasant weather, is a destination for end-of-season sporting events on both collegiate and high school levels. There are training camps at every level, including the pros. In light of this, there are a couple of months in March and April when booking fees can be well in excess of what I underwrote above.

This said, I would anticipate our range to be $13,500 per year on the absolute low end and $22,000 on the very high end. Remember, as of this writing we've only been at this for a few months and the jury, as they say, is still out. But, having gone through all of the numbers I am willing to use an assumption of $17,000 per year of EGI.

Expenses (Operating Costs)

After the initial expense of setting things up, which we will discuss in a later chapter, the only operating costs are about $50 per month of gratuity items, and the proportional utility cost, which comes out to about $60 per month. Here's the math:

Our house is a bit under 2,400 square feet. The Casita alone is 234 square feet. In other words, the Casita represents about 10% of the total square footage of the house. Our utility bills, which include water, sewer, garbage, gas, electric, cable TV, pool service, landscape, and pest control, average about $600 per month. Therefore, if we proportionally attribute all of the above expenses to the Casita's square footage (10%), then the Casita is responsible for paying about $60 per month of the utility costs:

$$\$600 \times 10\% = \$60/month$$

By adding the gratuity expenses to the utility expenses, we arrive at operating costs of about $110 per month, which is about $1,300 per year.

Turn-Labor Cost

As of now, I don't have any labor cost to allocate to cleaning/turns since I do it myself. Yep—the big shot investor, author, teacher, internet marketing guru Ben Leybovich turns his own Casita after his guests leave. Interestingly enough, when my seven year-old daughter comes out of her bath yelling that someone should clean the toilet because it is *awfully dirty*, yours truly does that as well!

It takes me about 50 minutes of primary time commitment per turn (I'll discuss this in more detail in the chapter on turns).

I do the turns myself for a couple of reasons:

1. I needed to understand the dynamics of what's involved so that I could systematize the process for when I am ready to source it out.

2. This is a house hack, not a business. If I buy more vacation rentals, which I may do sooner rather than later, I will, of course, outsource the turns turns. But, for those folks who need to save every penny, spending 50 minutes 5 times per month is certainly very reasonable considering the upside.

3. In Ohio, we had a lady helping us with some of the housekeeping chores, but my wife decided to hold off on it for our Arizona residence. Honestly, I would assume that before too long we will follow suit again, and when this happens, I'll include the Casita turns in our housekeeper's job description.

Understanding the Numbers

I debated whether to include this section. My intention, after all, is not to teach real estate investing in this book. I do that in the Cash Flow Freedom University. However, a house hack is a blend of that which is a place to live, with that which is a real estate investment. So, for those of you who may not have had exposure to REI, here come a few facts about how we do the numbers.

The cash-flow funnel looks like this:

Gross Scheduled Income (GSI) - when you own a property, you have to make some market-driven assumptions regarding how much revenue the property can generate in the best possible case. Think of this as the top-line scenario. As this applies to our Casita, that number is $25,325:

GSI = Booking Fees + Cleaning Fees = $23,725 + $1,600 = $25,325

GSI represents the absolute best-case scenario. This, my friends, does not happen in real estate too often.

Effective Gross Income (EGI) - After having made the necessary adjustments for our Casita, we arrived at what we felt was a reasonably conservative EGI assumption of $17,000.

I want you to pay attention to the delta between what's possible in the best case scenario (GSI), and what we feel is realistic (EGI). We dropped from $25,325 to $17,000…that's not pennies. This is a deduction for economic losses of about 35%. It's better to be safe than sorry!

Operating Expenses (OpEx) - From there, we subtracted all of the costs associated with running this Casita. Getting into an involved discussion around costs (and it would be involved) is not appropriate for this book, but I will mention two things.

One—debt service (mortgage payment) is not considered OpEx. And two—I did not include insurance because I'd be paying it with or without the Casita. In fact, one of the very obvious advantages of house hacking verses a dedicated rental of any sort is the shared (and therefore low) overhead, and this is one example.

So—the OpEx for our Casita, as we determined, is $1,300 per year.

Net Operating Income (NOI) - By subtracting the OpEx from the EGI, we arrive the Net Operating Income (NOI). This is a hugely important number in real estate investing because it tees up a lot of other numbers and rationale. For more information, please consult the CFFU. For our Casita this number is $15,700:

$$NOI = EGI - \text{Operating Costs} = \$17,000/year - \$1,300/year = \$15,700/year$$

Debt Service - Remember, this item was not included at the OpEx level. It comes into the equation at this point in order to arrive at the Cash Flow. However, the Casita doesn't have a mortgage, and therefore there isn't debt service.

Cash Flow (CF) - This is what's left after all income is in and all costs are out. In other words, this is what goes into your pocket. In our case, the CF seems to be around $1,300 per month:

$$CF = NOI - \text{Debt Service} = \$15,700 - \$0 = \$15,700/year$$
$$(\$1,308/\text{month average})$$

What this means is that we can project an average of $1,300 per month going into our pocket because of this Casita. Could it be less? Sure. Could it be more? Yes.

But, here's the thing—the P&I (principal & interest) payment on my house is just about $1,708 per month. The total PITI burn (principal, interest, taxes, insurance, and HOA) in 2017 is just about $2,050 per month. We touched on this earlier.

This means that our Casita is paying for all but $750 per month of our stay in this nice upscale home in the fastest growing county in the U.S. And if the goal is locational freedom, which a function of affordability, I am pretty comfortable in saying that $750 per month accomplishes it!

This Is a Blended House Hack

I keep harping at you that your house hack needs to be of a blended variety, which means it has to have both cash flow and equity appreciation components. Well, I don't want to spend too much time on this, but let's consider my house hack.

Call it conservative or call it scared, but I have learned that as exits go, there must be at least two. I've also learned that good cash flow always rests on solid equity appreciation, and solid equity appreciation is always underpinned by good cash flow. While this may be a bit counterintuitive to you, I would just ask you to believe me that when it comes to any variety of income property, what makes it a solid deal is that there is rationale for why the asset should appreciate over time.

As appreciation goes, there are two types: organic and forced. Organic appreciation is a function of the growth characteristics in the underlying marketplace. Forced appreciation, on the other hand, is the result of some combination of improvements to the physical asset and the operations that drive the market to recognize additional value in the asset due to better performance.

Both components are important because if you are banking on strictly organic appreciation, this is akin to gambling. No one has a crystal ball. While there may be a lot of logical underpinnings for continued growth, there are many unknown factors in the larger economy which can derail this growth. Banking on continued organic growth is how many people lost millions in the Great Recession.

On the other hand, in order to achieve forced appreciation there must be some amount of willingness in the overall marketplace to recognize our efforts and allocate additional value to our asset as a result. And this willingness to allocate value is usually indicative of confidence, which, in and of itself, is both the result of and the cause of continued growth.

I know this is a bit convoluted, but so is everything in real estate investing. The bottom line I need you to take away from this is that while organic appreciation is a bad tool on its own, it is a necessary tool for a successful investment.

Tying this all to my house hack, there are both types of appreciation working for us in some respect. On one hand, we live in the fastest growing county in the U.S. I am quite bullish on continued organic appreciation here. And, in addition, our house has some components of forced appreciation; hence we spent some money remodeling all of the baths, etc.

All things considered, we chose this particular house in lieu of something else specifically because we believed that it represented opportunities for cash flow and equity return. Therefore, by definition, ours is a Blended House Hack.

A Bit of Perspective on Our Casita House Hack

When most of you think about getting ahead financially, you likely lean toward the notion of tightening your belt, controlling your expenses, living frugally, etc.

This is mainstream messaging, and I am not going to tell you that it is always wrong. Indeed, at times, controlling expenses is exactly the right thing to do.

However, let us review what Patrisha and I have done with this house hack—and what you can do as well:

One: We went from burning $1,350 per month to live in a 1,560 square foot house in a town in Ohio that no one has ever heard of (for good reason) to burning just $750 to live in a house almost twice the size in the fastest growing county in the country for two years running, where there is sunshine and blue skies practically every day and where our kids attend the best school district in the U.S.

Two: We went from paying $1,250 per month for a 2nd floor 2 bedroom apartment to paying $750 per month for a great 2,400 square foot home with a pool in basically the same location. We've 10Xed our family's quality of life while lowering our burn by more than 50%.

The overriding point here is that lowering your cost of living doesn't necessarily mean tightening your belt, settling for less, and denying yourself all of the finer things in life. Sometimes, going after the finer things in life can in and of itself lower your cost of living, as we've proven with this house hack. We are in a much more expensive house, for less!

Yes, it does require a marginal shift in your thinking. It requires an ability to put things into perspective. And it requires not being afraid to zig while the mainstream zags! But, you can do it differently and better.

Let everyone else tighten their belts. Let them settle—you live as you need to live by passing the cost onto someone else!

The underlying premise of this book is that you can have anything you want as long as it makes you money. A house hack is one piece of that puzzle; it makes us money, and therefore we can have it.

Here's the thing—today, this house (where it is and what it is) represents heaven on earth for my family. It is literally everything we need and want. It enables our lives to be exactly what we want them to be today. But, when our life circumstances change and it becomes desirable to move to another location, don't you think we can do this all over?!

What I am describing to you, the process of creative house hacking such as we are doing it, represents locational freedom. An ability to say—I am done here; it's time to move on. If the whole point of this exercise is to achieve locational freedom, a properly executed house hack does it.

Final Thought

As I mentioned before, I've only been in this house for a few months. Perhaps I should have waited to write this book until I've lived here for 24 months. I just couldn't help myself. I feel that this house-hacking idea represents such a good solution for so many of you that I went ahead and wrote this book anyway!

Since I do not have trailing financial data for 24 months, I have to make some assumptions based on my understanding of the market dynamics. I think my assumptions are conservative and will stand the test of time. However, what if I am 50% wrong?

If I am 50% wrong, then instead of realizing cash flow of $1,300 per month, I'll be making $650. In this case, instead of $750 per month, my burn will be $1,400. I don't see this happening, but even if it did, I'd still only be paying $50 per month more to be here than what it cost me to live in Lima, Ohio. And I'd be here, where I want to be.

I'd say this represents the absolute worst-case scenario. And, I think it'd still be a WIN!

Chapter 6

House Hacking Is the Best Way for a Newbie to Invest in Real Estate!

This will be the shortest chapter in the book, but it is a power house! This may bust some dreams, and it will jump-start others. The choice is yours.

As real estate investing goes, I've been playing the game for over 10 years, having bought my first property in 2006. I lived through the 2008 Great Recession calamity, and I saw houses selling for 35% of new-build cost. I've seen friends of mine: smart people, entrepreneurial people, well-capitalized people, lose millions in the space of months. I have some perspective on the game; I definitely have a healthy respect for the power of the beast.

As I survey markets around the country in 2017, I am absolutely convinced that for some, if not most of you newbies, a well executed house hack is the best way to get into the real estate investing game.

Now—there are many books you can read which'll tell you that anyone can invest in real estate easily, with no money, and at any time. While in principle the information is often true, the Devil is in the details. Ultimately we do not operate in a vacuum, and we can only take what marketplace give us. Very few things work in the challenging 2017 cycle, and they all require rather extreme understanding of the sport.

On the other hand, a house hack makes things more manageable and more accessible, with more margin for error. It's the perfect spot to enter the game for a new investor!

Let's Talk Numbers to Underscore My Point

As we discussed, I am expecting about $15,700 of NOI to come out of my Casita. NOI, in case you forgot, stands for net operating income, which is income after operating expenses. And since I do not pay a mortgage on my Casita (it is wrapped into the house), the NOI is also the cash flow.

Here's the thing—if someone ever tells you that it's easy to achieve $1,300 of monthly cash flow from rental property, or even $1,000 of monthly cash flow, or even $300 of monthly cash flow, they are lying! There is nothing easy about any of it! Real estate investing is very, very difficult.

I promise you this—in ten years of doing it, this Casita represents far and away the easiest real estate cash flow I've ever created, period!

Furthermore, let us consider, for a minute, what it would actually take for me to buy $1,300 of cash flow in dedicated investment assets. In other words, if I were going to buy assets to replace this $1,300 per month of cash flow, what would that involve?

Follow My Logic

As you remember from earlier, the formula for Cash Flow is:

$$CF = NOI - Debt\ Service$$

And the formula for the NOI is essentially:

$$NOI = Income - Operating\ Costs$$

The formula for the value based on income is:

$$Value = NOI\ /\ Market\ Capitalization\ Rate$$

Now, follow me:

What we are trying to do in this exercise is establish approximately how much I'd have to pay for a piece of investment real property capable of replacing $1,300 per month of cash flow from my Casita. In order to do this, I must establish the likely NOI for such an investment asset, and then I'll be able to capitalize that NOI into likely value based on the known market Capitalization Rate.

Since we know the cash flow ($1,300), all we need to do in order to estimate the NOI is add the debt service payment to the cash flow:

IF: $CF = NOI - Debt\ Service$

THEN: $NOI = CF + Debt\ Service$

So, what is the likely debt service for an investment vehicle capable of providing $1,300 per month of CF? Well, this amount can vary, and I don't want to get into the woods of real estate investing rationale here, so I would ask you to believe me when I tell you that it won't be any less than about $2,500 per month. In other words, if I were to make a down payment and finance the rest of the acquisition on a piece of real estate capable of generating $1,300 per month of cash flow, I would more than likely realize a mortgage payment of $2,500 per month.

This means that in order to achieve CF of $1,300 per month, I'd need NOI of $3,800 on a monthly basis:

$$NOI = CF + Debt\ Service = \$1,300/month + \$2,500/month = \$3,800/month$$

At this point, I am going to use some more fancy real estate investment jargon, which will make complete sense to those of you who live and breath real estate (like me), and no sense at all to others. If you are lost, go here and study the Cash Flow Freedom University

If the NOI an asset is capable of producing is $3,800 per month, or $45,600 per year, then in a marketplace exhibiting valuations at a 10% capitalization rate, the value of the underlying asset capitalizes to $456,000:

$$Value = NOI\ /\ Market\ Cap\ Rate$$

$$Value = \$45,600\ /\ 10\% = \$456,000$$

$456,000—this is how much a reasonably aggressive investor willing to deploy capital at a rate of return of 10% would have to pay for a building capable of generating $1,300 per month of cash flow. It's what

I would have to pay in order to replace my Casita cash flow of $1,300 in a 10% Cap Rate marketplace.

But, in 2017, there are no marketplaces left that anyone has ever heard of where real estate trades at a 10% Cap—at least not any real estate that's worth owning. Even little Lima, Ohio, positioned perfectly between a cornfield and a railroad track, is at trading at about 8.5% now for quality assets! So, if you can find a solid 8% Cap, you can consider yourself golden.

The problem relative to me replacing my Casita cash flow is that paying an 8% Cap for $45,600 of NOI means spending a cool $570,000.

Guys and gals—I got this Casita for free. It came with the darn house.

Let me say this again to make sure it sinks in:

I Got This Casita for Free!!!!!

I am not paying any additional debt service on it because there was no additional debt—period. What a freaking gift!

Are you with me?

What do you think is easier: buying a 10-unit complex for $570,000 or doing a house hack as we did? Let's bullet-point this:

> Buying the 10-unit complex would require a down-payment of at least 25%, which is $142,500 based on purchase price of $570,000. The Casita required no additional down-payment outside of the 5% I put down on the house.
> Buying the 10-unit complex would require taking on an additional $427,500 of debt. The Casita required no additional debt.
> The 10-unit complex would require paying additional property taxes. The Casita does not.
> The 10-unit complex would require additional management infrastructure. The Casita does as well, but it's infinitely easier.

Let us set aside the fact that you may not have $142,500 to put down on an investment property, and the fact that you may have serious trouble qualifying for the debt. And let us ignore the fact that managing a 10-unit complex does indeed require some skills, which many of you don't have.

Set aside all of that, what you are left with is that both of these investments are capable of producing the same cash flow, but one is so much easier to do than the other. Why is this even a contest?!

And Then There's This!

If the reason you want to be a real estate investor is because you think it'll lead you to some freedom, then a house hack is the most straightforward answer. Why? Because if you do it the way I am teaching you here, you will automatically buy your locational freedom. You will buy yourself the ability to move around freely. What could be more intrinsic to freedom than that?!

So—it's your life and it's your call as to how you want to play it. But, I imagine that for a lot of you, a solid house hack is indeed the best real estate investment you can make at any time, but especially in 2017!

Chapter 7

How Much Income Tax Will I Pay on Vacation Rental Income?

OK, this is a loaded subject and highly individual in nature. I will not be offering any specific advice here, only providing some framework for your further research. Having said that, there's this:

Disclaimer: *I am not a CPA or a licensed financial adviser. All information herein is for educational and entertainment purposes only. Before taking action please seek advice from licensed professionals.*

About Income

Something a lot of people miss about their finances is that while it does matter how much you earn, what matters much more is how much you keep of what you earn. For example, if your salary is $200,000 but you pay a 50% effective tax rate, then your spendable income is only $100,000. On the other hand, if your income is $125,000, but your effective tax rate is only 8%, you are actually left with more spendable cash ($115,000). See the dichotomy? These two scenarios are completely real and not hypothetical.

Indeed, all income is not equal. Some types of income are considered earned, while other types of income are deemed passive. The importance of this distinction resides in the fact that different types of incomes are taxed differently, making them more or less advantageous from an effective tax rate point of view.

I don't want to spend a lot of time on this, but we do need some context to discuss taxation of the income from your house hack. So, let's touch on the highlights.

3 Types of Income

There are three types of income, and they are *earned, passive,* and *portfolio.*

Earned Income

Think of earned income as any income that requires a trade of your time for money. Essentially, if the way you generate income is by showing up at the office five days per week, your income is earned. Also, if you are an independent contractor, you still trade time for money. As such, your income also lands in the earned-income bucket.

Now, an employee reports earned income to the IRS through a W2, while an independent contractor reports earned income through a 1099, but they are both earned and both are subject to FICA taxes such as Medicare and Social Security, though it works a little differently.

The bottom line, however, is that earned income is, unfortunately, very highly taxcd.

<u>Portfolio and Passive Income</u>

Both of these types of income are generated via investments of some sort. Portfolio income is generally long-term income from paper investments, such as dividends from stocks, interest from trusts, etc. Capital gain on the sale of paper assets is also considered a form of portfolio income. Passive income is gencrally income from rental real estate

The line between passive and portfolio income is a little blurry. The important piece is that while these are taxed at your income tax bracket, they are not subject to any of the FICA taxes. Just right there, you save yourself at least 15% of your money right off the bat! And this is not even accounting for many other benefits that you receive that are associated with this type of income. There are numerous reasons for you to education yourself on this matter, and the entire discussion lies outside of the scope of this book, so let's move on.

Now that we touched on the basics, I have to disappoint you. Unfortunately, while the guidelines are not very clear there is a better than 50/50 chance that the income from your Cash Flow House Hack will be viewed by the IRS as earned income which is subject not only to the income tax at the appropriate tax-bracket but is also subject to FICA taxes.

This means, for example, that if—after expenses—you report $15,000 of house-hacking income, in a year when you find yourself in the 25% income tax bracket, you will need to pay $3,750 of income tax on your house hacking income plus another roughly $2,250 (15%) of FICA taxes, for a total tax exposure of $6,000:

Income Tax (25%): $15,000 x 25% = $3,750

FICA Taxes* (15%): $15,000 x 15% = $2,250

Total Tax Exposure = Income Tax + FICA Taxes = $3,750 + $2,250 = $6,000

Now that's what I call a bite, wouldn't you agree?

*FICA taxes are actually 15.3%, but just to keep things simple I use 15% throughout this book.

What Can You Do to Pay Less Tax?

You can't lie to the IRS. They can hurt you in a big way!

That said, there are things that you can do!

<u>Buy the Right Kind of House</u>

From the standpoint of taxes, it's important to understand that, in general, any part of the house which serves as office space for you can be deducted on your taxes. It is important to mention that a space "must be used EXCLUSIVELY and REGULARLY for home office space" for the IRS to allow it (i.e., you can't claim your dining room table as your home office).

You can deduct what's called *direct expenses*, which are things like repairs, paint, flooring, and other expenses related to setting up and maintaining your office. And you can also deduct *indirect expenses*, which are prorated based on square footage and can be items such as mortgage interest, property taxes, utilities, prorated general home repairs, etc.

For indirect expenses, we have to follow something called *Personal Use Rule* which says that if you use your home for more than 14 days for personal use, you have to start to prorate the days as well as the square footage.

Thus, if you live in a 2,500 square foot house where your office is 250 square feet (which represents 10% of the overall size) then in theory you can deduct a 10% proration of all applicable indirect expenses. Because 100% of the time the use of that space is as an office you don't have to do anything more. Clearly, the bigger the percentage that your office represents, the more advantageous the deductions come tax time.

However, in your zealousness, don't get too creative and try to claim that the 800-square-foot room which houses your office desk, a pool table, TV, wet bar with stools, and two couches is your office. Understand, there is a litmus test for what is an office and what's not. The room I just described sounds like anything but an office. Unless throwing parties in your house is the nature of your business, this room is not an office and you will get red flagged.

This deduction business works a bit differently for a vacation rental, as I will explain in a bit, but as you should begin to see, the layout of your house hack is the key to how much square footage you'll be able to claim as business related.

In my house hack, for example, there are two rooms that are quite obviously good candidates for deductions. First, our office above the garage, which is about 450 square feet and has nothing in it aside from the desk, filing cabinets, and one sofa. All of Patrisha's real estate signs are stored there as well as all of my recording and podcasting equipment. The entry into the room is not from inside of the main house but, as we discussed earlier, via a staircase on the outside. Finally, the room is under lock and key.

There is no argument. This is as straightforward as it gets—this is an office. There's no possibility of red flags here.

Aside from the office, there is the Casita itself, which is 234 square feet. Now—since we obviously have friends and family who stay in this Casita a few weeks out of the year, I cannot claim 100% of prorated write-off on this square footage. As I mentioned above, the *Personal Use Rule* states that if I use the space for any more than 14 days out of the year, I have to prorate the days as well as the square footage.

I would imagine that the Casita is either used as a rental or is vacant in between guests at least 90% of the time, meaning I use it for personal use 10% of the time. To keep the math simple let's just take 90% of the square footage and write-off 215. That's not exactly how the CPA will do it, but it's close enough.

Adding the 450 square feet of the office and the 215 square feet of the Casita gives us total deductible square footage of about 665, which represents over 25% of the entire house!

I will let my CPAs tell me what to do, but if I am anywhere near to being correct on this math, I should be able to write off a substantive proportion of my indirect expenses, which is all going to shield Casita income from taxes.

Question: Do you think that when I looked for my house hack, the notion of maximizing deductible square footage was an important component to me?

Answer: Hell yes! I knew I'd be generating income with this house hack, and would need all of the deductions that I could muster.

Not just any house works well for a house hack. Keep reading!

Entity Formation

The other part of the answer may stem from the above explanation of passive and portfolio income. All of this is incredibly oversimplified and overly generalized, so be sure to seek out specific advice from licensed professionals, but here's the gist.

When you own a company and you work in this company as one of the employees, you can take money out of that company as both the employee and the owner. As we discussed above, the money which you earn as the employee will indeed be subject to both the income tax and all applicable payroll taxes. However, the income you get from this company as the owner is considered either a dividend (in the case of a C Corporation) or an owner's distribution (in the case of an S Corporation). In either case, though, there will not be any payroll taxes associated with that income.

So, let's get back to our example.

Assume again that your house hack earned you $15,000 in a year. But, let's say the money went into your company first and then was distributed to you. Let's call your corporation an S Corp. As such, you are taking the money out of this S Corp as both the employee and the owner.

103

You will have to get qualified advice from your CPA on all of this, but let's assume, for example purposes, that out of that $15,000, you took $8,000 as the employee and the rest as the owner's distribution:

Total Income:	$15,000
W2 income:	$8,000
Distribution (Schedule E):	$7,000

In this case, if we continue to assume an income tax rate for you of 25%, the taxation would look like this:

W2 Income Total:	$8,000
Earned Income Tax (25%):	$2,000
Earned Income FICA (15%)	$1,200

Total Tax Exposure of W2 Income = Income Tax + FICA Tax =
$2,000 + $1,200 = $3,200

Now, the distribution:

Total Distribution:	$7,000
Income Tax (25%):	$1,750
FICA Tax:	N/A

Total tax Exposure of Distribution Income is $1,750.

So, the $8,000 you take out of the company as W2 income will cost you a total of $3,200 in taxes. And, the $7,000 you take as distribution will cost you a total of $1,750 in taxes. Add those together, and by taking the income via an S Corporation your total exposure is $4,950.

Total Tax Exposure = W2 taxes + Distribution Taxes = $3,200 + $1,750 = $4,950

Now, if you remember from a couple of paragraphs above, you initially were going to need to pay $6,000 in taxes by taking all of the house-hack income directly. Thus, going through a corporation lowers your exposure by $1,050, which represents a savings in the neighborhood of 17.5%. Do you think you could work with that?!

One other point to add here is with regard to how much W2 wage you should pay yourself in an S Corporation. Some of you may be thinking: *if I don't have to pay FICA taxes on distributions, why not take $1,000 of wages and $14,000 as distribution?* The IRS requires you to take a "reasonable wage". What is a reasonable wage? Here is more information: https://www.irs.gov/uac/wage-compensation-for-s-corporation-officers

Conclusion

When it comes to tax planning, what I've covered here barely scratches the surface, as they say. I've illustrated only a sliver of what can be done. My final thought for this chapter is this: the tax code in the United States is and always will be geared toward those who want to create their freedom, not toward those who try to earn it! So, go hunting!

And as always, seek the advice of a good CPA!

Part 3:
What You Need to Know to Get it Done Right

Chapter 8

How Do I Choose the Best Location to House Hack?

Okay—now that you understand the overriding philosophy of the house hack and have somewhat of a grasp on the numbers, the remainder of the book is devoted to answering specific questions relative to the process.

Let's start with the most obvious question—how do I choose the best location for a Blended House Hack?

Aside from the quite obvious notion that you are doing this in a place that makes your heart sing, in other words, you are doing this for *you* and whatever *your* reasons are, there are some things to think through here.

This House Is Not Just for You!

Here's the thing—it is hard enough to find a location that works for your family's needs and wants, but when house hacking, you have to consider not only your needs and likes, but everyone else's as well. This is tricky!

While it is true that you will live there for some period of time, what you also must do is attract other people to your house hack, right? Whether the essence of the hack is equity, requiring you to find a buyer, or cash flow, requiring you to find a tenant/guest, unless people are attracted to this house hack's location, the strategy fundamentally doesn't work.

Therefore, as you are considering a location, you have to give weight to what the "masses" think. I've said it before and I'll say it again—*buying real estate is no more difficult than falling out of a tree. Buying the right kind of real estate...now that is a challenge!*

Location, Location, Location

Location is the single most determining element impacting the overall desirability of real property. This is always true. People are attracted to certain locations for good reasons, and to succeed at a house hack, you need to understand those reasons. I know this might be basic, but just to be sure that we are all on the same page let's review some basic truths for assessing desirability in real estate.

5 Considerations for Property Location

Growth Market

There is really no other way but to be blunt here. While many things are possible in all markets, there are simply more profit opportunities in a growth market. Growth markets are that way for a reason. New employers are coming in and existing employers are expanding operations. Employees are following the jobs. The tax base is growing, which likely means the place is cleaner and better amenitized. As more people permanently relocate, more visitors come to town to visit them. And as they come, even more amenities become available. And so on and so forth.

This growth dynamic is good for all sorts of real estate. While it is undoubtedly more difficult to find a discount in a growth market, the efforts can pay off much bigger than in other places.

So, to start with, as a general rule of thumb we would have to agree that a house hack works best in a market that can be characterized as a growth market. More job growth, more population growth, more buyers, more tenants—these are all good things.

Distance from Work

This is one of the basics—you probably don't want to drive for two hours to get to work. Let me put it to you differently: even if you were to find the most serene piece of dirt on Earth, with the most beautiful house with gold-plated toilets, as much as you might want to buy it because it makes you feel special, you won't buy it if it would mean a 2-hour drive to work.

One of the main factors determining where people want to live is proximity to where they work and make money. Not everyone can do what Ben Leybovich does, which is sit in a nice leather chair in his living room (or a lounge chair by the pool) and work on his laptop and cell phone as he pleases. Most people go to their *job*. We need to understand the realities of this as they relate to our house hacks, and it doesn't much matter which type of hack you decide to pursue.

Generally speaking, we have to buy in proximity to large employment centers.

Well-rated Schools

I don't know that anything really needs to be said here. Patrisha and I specifically moved because of the school for our kids. Everything else is very nice, but it's just a bonus. I don't think it's unreasonable to assume that children's educational infrastructure is high on the list of factors when choosing a location to buy a house in.

Live & Play Infrastructure

When Patrisha and I lived in Lima, we drove every single week for 2 hours (one way) to get to Whole Foods Market and a Kumon center for our kids in Dayton. This wasn't because we had nothing better to do with our time. It was because Dayton was the closest location to us. If this doesn't describe both a lack of infrastructure and an uncomfortable lifestyle, I don't know what does.

By contrast, now that we live in Chandler, Arizona, we've got four organic grocery stores within 12 minutes from our house. There is one WholeFoods and three Sprouts Markets. Kumon centers are literally on every corner here. Movie theatres, shopping, restaurants, parks—you name it. Our choices are endless and immediately available.

Which location do you think makes for a better house hack? People like conveniences...period. The closer your house hack is to the things people like to do, the easier your job of selling it to your audience will be. And, once again, it doesn't matter much whether we are talking about an Equity House Hack, a Cash Flow House Hack, or both.

Vacation - Getaway

While this is a niche audience, vacationers are a very real audience. I've spent the last 27 years in the Midwest, and for me the realities of a marketplace that attracts vacationers were totally foreign prior to a year ago. Just ask yourself—who goes to the Midwest unless they have to, let alone to take a vacation?! Seriously, unless looking at a smokestack or cornstalks is your idea of nirvana, you don't usually consider the Midwest a vacation spot! The two reasons you'll go there are on business or you have family to visit there. Otherwise, people leave the Midwest to go on vacation, not the other way around.

While still in Ohio, I remember talking to some of my real-estate friends who happened to own property in growth markets. They were telling me how much money they were making with vacation rentals. I remember just drawing blanks...how in the hell can I put a duplex in Lima on AirBnB...who'll want it, and why?

So tell me, would it be advantageous (especially from a cashflow perspective) to be house hacking in a destination location? Would that offer you some options that you wouldn't otherwise have?

Yes! Done.

Retire - Really Get Away :)

Retirees used to be a niche audience, but have you checked recently to see the numbers behind the retiring baby-boomers? How many baby-boomers retire every day, would you think?

The answer: 8,000 - 10,000 baby-boomers retire every day. Check out this article from The Washington Post if you don't believe me!

No—not every baby-boomer will relocate to a nicer climate upon retiring, but enough of them will. Do you think it might not be a bad idea to own some property in locations they might want to relocate to?

I've had two experiences lately which, in my mind, sum this whole situation up. First—the third party to stay in our Casita was a retired couple who came down for 7 nights. They were here to finalize the building specs for the house they are looking to retire in.

Two weeks after their stay, my parents came to visit. Based on my conversations with them, I am pretty sure they expected to come off the airplane straight into the desert, and their biggest expected worry in life would be not to fall on a cactus or pass out from heat exhaustion.

But then they got here, and the blue skies happened. Greenery all over the place happened. Manicured highways happened. The palm trees along almost every road happened. My pool, and my shaded courtyard, happened. All of this happened, and now my wife, the realtor, is looking for a house for them. They've since bough one…See what I mean?

So - Where Is The Best Place to House Hack?

This answer is simple—you want to be both in a growth market and in a location which best synthesizes all 5 of the reasons people buy property:

- ❏ It's close to work
- ❏ It's close to good schools
- ❏ It's close to recreation
- ❏ It's in a desirable vacation spot
- ❏ It's a desirable retirement destination

It is not easy to truly synthesize all of these elements in one place. Thankfully, you don't really need all of the above in the mix. As long as there are enough of these things working, the house hack should work!

Our House Hack

Well, aside for the BASIS Charter Schools, which were very much integral to us choosing Chandler, the first macroeconomic point to make is that Maricopa County is the fastest growing county in the U.S. for two years straight. That tells you something. The population growth is high here for a number of reasons.

Snowbirds are notorious for retiring here and likely will continue to do so. In fact, after Florida, Arizona is likely the second-most-prolific retirement destination.

Along the same lines, Arizona is a vacation destination—not to mention that because the weather is so good for most of the year, every collegiate and high-school sporting event you can think of holds their finals here. Sporting events are huge here!

And then there's the employment-base growth. I see so many people moving from California, which is predicated on corporations and tech start-ups moving from California. My house is about 10 minutes away from Intel, for instance. The Price Corridor which houses Wells Fargo, PayPal, and everyone in between, is also about 10 minutes away.

Did I get lucky in that Chandler represents such a synergy of good weather, educational opportunities for my kids, retirement destination, vacation spot, and good old-fashioned employment base growth?

Yes—it is fortunate for me that Chandler has all of these things. However, I would not call it lucky. This is what I was specifically looking for. Before deciding on Arizona, we traveled to many places. Some made it pretty high on our list of possible locations to pursue. But, at the end of the day, moving to Arizona was a calculated decision based on the very synergy of all of the aspects of desirability.

Now, do you have to have all of these in order to succeed? No. You could just go after retirees or just after vacationers. But, being able to offer something for everyone is simply priceless.

Chapter 9

What Kind of House Works Best for House Hacking?

Introduction

As you know by now, as house hacks go there are 3 types. Equity House Hacking places all of the focus entirely on the equity appreciation. Cash Flow House Hacking focuses on using the rental income to offset the monthly burn. And Blended House Hacking focuses on both, in that while we want the income to offset the expense of living there, we also want elements of both forced and organic appreciation.

What Kind of House Works Best for the Equity House Hack?

I don't want to spend too much time on this for a couple of reasons. For one thing, I did not choose to pursue this route for myself for reasons I already described in an earlier chapter, most of which have to do with risk. Even in my real estate investing career over the last decade, I've tended to shy away from pursuing retail fix and flipping due to its heightened risk profile. I don't like to preach that which I don't practice, and so I am not the best person to explain the minutiae. I certainly understand the strategy, but my friends Brian Burke or Darren Sager, who do this kind of thing for a living, are much better equipped to teach you the finer points.

Just as a very generalized description, akin to a bird's-eye view from 10,000 feet, here are three bullet-points you should internalize:

1. Buy a house in a really desirable location in order to have the best chance of organic price inflation. People buy primarily the location and secondarily the house itself. Putting a great house in an undesirable location is a cardinal sin, specifically when your entire model rests on being able to sell well, as it does in an Equity House Hack.

2. Buy a house without functional obsolescence which can't be remedied cost effectively. Functional obsolescence is a term that describes outdated structural elements in a house that prevent the house from functioning as a reasonable buyer would expect. Some examples of functional obsolescence are a four-bedroom house with one bath; a garage-door opening that is only 5 feet tall and cannot be fixed easily; a bedroom which is accessed only through another bedroom. The issue with some of these is not that they can't be

fixed but that the amount of money it takes to fix them far exceeds that which the value of the house can support. Stay away from that.

3. Buy the house cheap enough so that you can afford to do a quality rehab.

Haha—nothing much to it...simple as that.

Not really, though. My friend, Brian Burke, of Praxis Capital, who's done a few hundred of these fix and flips, and Darren Sager, who flips luxury homes in New jersey because he thinks it's fun, will tell you that while what I described is true, the complexity of what's involved is staggering. They are right.

The thing that is most bothersome and cannot be overstated is the exit risk on an Equity House Hack. In order to maximize your return on this strategy, you will need to live in this house for two years, because after two years the capital gains tax on the sale goes down to zero. This can be a huge advantage. But, two years is infinity in terms of market dynamics.

In 2008 all of us saw how, within 12 months, the market absolutely collapsed. Imagine a situation whereby you are 4 months away from placing your hack on the market, and all of a sudden prices collapse by 12%, 20%, 40%! You can't sell, which means you have to carry this thing toward the back side of the market correction, which could take years. And remember—there is no income component here. You are paying for that entire burn!

This is straight from my real estate investing teachings, but it very much applies. I am of the school of thought that our number one objective should always be to not lose, and only once that has been well underwritten do we need to worry about making money.

The lacking income component on an Equity House Hack represents more risk than I was willing to take, so I opted instead for a Blended House Hack.

<u>Final Thought</u>

Now—before bringing this section to a close, I must place a small asterisk on Equity House Hacks, and this requires me to eat some of the words I've written above. Here's the deal: it is in fact possible to manufacture income in a house which is meant as an Equity House Hack. I briefly alluded to this before. All you have to do is share your house with a roommate. I have several students who are doing this. They are renting out one or even two bedrooms in their 4-bedroom houses and allowing shared use of the common areas.

For some of you, this may be a solution. The running theme, however, is that everyone who manages to pull this off (at least those people whom I know of) are either single, or a couple without children. These are young professionals. They make good money, and they want to be smart with it. They don't have children, and they are not opposed to having like-minded people renting from them and sharing common areas. To put it simply—these guys won't say no to a good party...lol.

Personally, this describes the opposite of what I want in life. I appreciate those of you who can hack it this way, but I don't want people in my space...not only because I don't really think it's safe, but because I just don't want people in my space. I don't want to stay up late with anyone other than my wife. I don't want to party into the night. I don't want to open my refrigerator and find fluffy stuff growing on someone's pizza from the week prior. I don't want to smell those nasty microwavable dinners throughout my house. And (this is big), I sure as all hell don't want to hear people getting their groove on at the other end of the hallway!

None of that appeals to me, not even if I can get $1,000 per month toward my mortgage payment out of this deal. I don't want that even if my roommate pays for the entire mortgage.

So, if you ask me, while I can see how buying a regular old 4-bedroom house can indeed work for some people, in my opinion it is the wrong type of an asset if you want income.

What Kind of House Works Best for a Blended House Hack?

My house in Chandler is a Blended House Hack, whereby the income comes via vacation-rental bookings. The footprint of our house lends itself perfectly to the vacation-rental model.

Again, I don't want to spend much time discussing the equity side of this equation, just understand that it's there. A few brief thoughts:

- ❏ We spent a total of about $30,000 on the rehab.
- ❏ The Casita rehab cost $8,000. The rest of the money went into the main house.
- ❏ We replaced all of the bath countertops (2 in addition to the Casita) with granite. We installed upgraded under hung sinks and high grade fixtures.
- ❏ We ran travertine tub surround in the kid's bath.
- ❏ In the master bath, we pulled out the shower/tub combo and created a fantastic travertine shower with multiple showerheads.

Aside from being located in an area that is more likely than not to experience organic price inflation for years to come (this is the organic appreciation), the updates I just mentioned should increase the desirability of our house hack and help it sell for more. This is the essence of the "blended" in our Blended House Hack.

However, the beauty of this is in the fact that if I am wrong about the marketplace and we end up needing to keep this house longer than I thought, it's all good with me because of the income component. The house is incredibly cheap to own due to the income from the Casita, so we'll stay as long as we need to in order for the market to cooperate.

So, let's move on to the elements supporting the income in this house hack.

The Perfect Footprint

I happen to think that my house is an absolutely perfect house from the standpoint of generating cash flow, so the rest of the chapter is devoted to a discussion of all of the attributes that make it so.

Naturally, please understand that I'm not trying to tell you to go find my exact floor-plan for your house hack. That's not likely, nor is it necessary. I am, however, excited to share with you all of the attributes and characteristics that make my house so great for a house hack so that you can look for a house of your own that will offer you comparable benefits. I am confident that, if you search hard enough, you'll find some version of them in any market!

Main Entry

Okay—I got a little lucky with how perfect this is. When we began our search, the only thing I clearly understood was that because we'd be renting out part of the house, safety and privacy were absolutely paramount. I had no idea what that actually meant in terms of the floor-plan or foundation foot-print, but what we actually ended up with has surpassed all of our expectations.

This is really cool for a house hack. There are two ways to enter my house. One entryway is through the garage, but the other is via an iron security gate in the front (see the image below). The gate is under lock and key, which makes it ideal for making sure that while our guests can get in, people who shouldn't have access don't.

Image A: Front Elevation

The gate makes this the most secure house I've ever lived in. Literally, entering the premises requires ringing the doorbell, which is wired into the main house with an intercom. And, to top it off, from a large living room window, which you can kind of see hiding behind a tree on the picture above, there is direct line of sight toward the gate.

From an owner's perspective, the level of privacy this whole setup creates cannot be overstated! And guests like this setup because, like me, they enjoy the security of knowing that no one will be able to enter who isn't supposed to. As a matter of fact, one of the most often asked questions relative to vacation rentals is exactly this—*how private is the Casita?* It is so easy to address this concern with our Casita.

Private Entrance into the Casita

Along with the safety question, I get this one—*Is there a private entrance?*

Once guests enter the iron gate, they find themselves in a quaint courtyard.

Image B: Courtyard

What you are looking at (and don't laugh at the quality) is a panoramic shot of the courtyard I took with my fancy iPhone. This is exactly the view that opens up to the guests once they walk through the gate and underneath a castle-like arch.

Now let's be honest—this may not be the absolute most attractive or the most scenic corner of the world, but this is not too bad. It is certainly inviting and pleasant. And, it's very photogenic, which is important and something I'll discuss later.

On the left is the entrance to the main living quarters. The knee-wall that you can kind of see is the staircase leading to the 2nd-floor office I discussed earlier. And on the right (the patio door) is the Casita.

The footprint of the house is loosely the shape of a horse shoe. As you look at the house from the vantage point in the picture above, the main house is in the left wing, and it extends depth-wise into the back of the lot. The garage and the Casita are both in the right wing. There are two important functional consequences of such a footprint:

One: The Casita has a separate entrance, which is important for obvious reasons. The not-so-obvious benefit is that while the entrance into the Casita is separate, it is not so hidden from my view that I would be unaware of some monkey business going on. It's my house, and while I don't want my guests too close, neither do I want them too far. This is important in an owner-occupied house hack!

Two: As you can see, the Casita is attached to the house by way of a garage wall but does not share any walls with the main living quarters. In one of the earlier chapters, I mentioned that upon arriving in Chandler we had looked for a duplex but that there just aren't any that fit the bill. This house is a better situation than a duplex could ever be. Think about this: in a side-by-side duplex we would necessarily be sharing walls with our tenants, and in a stacked duplex we'd be sharing a floor or ceiling. In either case—what a pain in the ears that could end up being...we don't have this issue in our house!

The courtyard separating the main house from the Casita measures about 25 feet across. What a perfect footprint. We are separated from our guests by 25 feet of exterior space and share no walls. Literally, we don't hear them, and they don't hear us—period. This is what I call a perfect footprint for a Cash Flow House Hack!

Size of Rental Unit (this is important)

Here comes a little more of my real estate investing philosophy, but it's relevant.

What is most important to understand is that the size of the rental unit in large part defines who the prospective tenant base will be. If what you have is a one-bedroom unit, you are not going to be attractive to groups of 9. Vice versa, if you are renting out a 2,300 square foot house with 4 bedrooms and 3 baths, you are not likely to attract couples or business travelers.

To put this differently, if you do not want a group of 9 people living next door to you, then don't bring to market a 2,300 square foot unit with 4 bedrooms and 3 baths.

Are Larger Units a Problem?

It depends on the market. But, certain realities just are what they are in any market:

- ❏ This is a house hack, which means that your guests will literally be coming and going in and out of your space. So—do you want groups of five, seven, or nine people coming and going in and out of your space?
- ❏ Do you think that wear and tear on a 234 square foot Casita capable of accommodating parties of one or two will be lighter than wear and tear on a house capable of accommodating parties of nine?

Does all of that make sense to you? Remember—it's not all about how much you earn. What's left after expenses is more important. And as far as that goes, every aspect of ownership becomes more expensive directly proportionally to property size. So, unless going bigger generates so much more revenue that it's worth it, then why bother? And this is exactly where we run into conflict!

Go on AirBnB right now and check out prices. What you'll discover is that the premium you can charge for rent on a 2-bedroom versus a 1-bedroom is usually very minimal, making the per square foot rent quite a bit lower on a 2-bedroom. If you can buy a 2-bedroom for the same price as the 1-bedroom, go for it. If nothing else having the second bedroom will give you more options. But, if you have to pay a bunch more for that 2-bedroom, you should really consider carefully.

In our case, for example, the Casita is 13 feet x 18 feet, or 234 square feet. It has a bath and a kitchenette. We book the Casita for $65 per night, whereas there are 1,800 square foot houses on VRBO that are going for $145. This means that for almost eight times the square footage, they are getting only about twice the rent. Put it differently, while we get $0.28 per square foot per night, they get $0.08, and that's just the top line. Once we start talking about the operating costs, this delta becomes much more exacerbated.

And did I mention that we got our Casita for free...it came with the house!

Are you getting this?

When We Bought

On the day we took possession of the house, the Casita looked like this:

Image C: Casita Interior Prior to Remodel

You can't tell from this picture, but those are 9-foot ceilings and 8-foot solid-core, heavy doors. Even as it was, the space did not feel cramped or cheap. While we don't want any more space than need be, less space than what is practical is not good either. This space seemed to just make the cut.

The door on the left was a walk-in closet, while the door on the right is the bath, which before the remodel looked like this:

Image D: Casita Bath Before Remodel

If this were going to be a typical long-term rental, the fit and finish would have been just fine as it sat. For a vacation rental, however, Patrisha and I thought we'd be better off with higher-end finishing textures. I will discuss this remodel in detail in a later chapter, but just a few thoughts to lay the foundation.

If you log onto VRBO or any of the other platforms, you'll see that there is a category of rentals titled "private room." Not surprisingly, considering our discussion around all of those people trying to create cash flow in their otherwise Equity House Hacks, lots and lots of listings can be found there in the range of $30 - $35 per night. These are simply spare bedrooms being rented out in a straightforward SFR. These likely represent the bottom end of the spectrum.

The other choice travelers have available to them is, of course, a hotel. This is the other end of the spectrum. But, about $145 per night is what it takes in our location to book any hotel remotely resembling something "nice." Rates go up from there.

And now that we have defined the opposite ends of the spectrum, here comes some more investment rationale. Most people think that when we make our units nicer, it is for one reason only—to get more rent revenue. While this is true, and we are often able to get premium on our rents for units with upgraded finishing textures, the thing to always remember is that how much income we get is less important than how much of it we keep after expenses. And in this way, we are very sensitive to what type of expenses we'll have to contend with...and how we can minimize them.

The thing to understand is this:

Some of the line-items under the category *expenses* are the result of people's behavior. Whether we get paid on time, whether they clean up before leaving, whether they are kind toward the unit or trash it: these are all function of people's behavior! And while there can never be any absolutes in this world, some tenants and guests are definitely more likely to leave a mess after themselves and cost you more than others.

The logic goes like this:

    A. By making our Casita a bit nicer and better amenitized, we can achieve higher booking fees.

    B. Higher booking fees will lead to attracting better qualified guests who have more discretionary income. Why? Because less qualified guests with less discretionary income will tend to opt for lower priced rentals (such as those $30 per night spare bedrooms).

    C. Higher-qualified guests who are willing to pay more are less likely to trash our Casita, or be a nuisance.

Again, there are no absolutes in life, but my experience tells me that this is right on. There is, of course, a caveat and it is this: the market ultimately decides what things are worth. Could it happen that after spending the extra money to make the Casita extra nice, we are still unable to garner higher booking fees? Absolutely, and therein lies the danger of value-add. If this happens, the joke's on us.

However, having researched the marketplace, we thought we could pull it off, but to do so we'd need to install a little kitchenette. We felt that at $65 per night, our Casita would need to compete favorably with a $220 hotel unit, and we needed a kitchenette for that!

So, we took the door off of the closet, opened the walls, ran the plumbing into the bath on the other side of the wall, installed a sink-base with granite countertop to match the one we put into the bathroom, installed a small stainless sink, and a couple of uppers with a shelf for the microwave. And next to the sink-base there was enough room for a small fridge. And suddenly we had a gorgeous little kitchenette!

Having done the work we ended up with something quite nice!

Image D: Casita Remodeled Bath

Image F: Casita Remodeled Interior

We will discuss the remodel in more detail in a later chapter.

One Thing Not to Do

The beautiful thing about real estate is that the phrase "different folks, different strokes" really does apply. There are so many ways to make money, and there are so many ways to approach buying the perfect house for a house hack.

Hopefully in this chapter I've given you some ideas as to what a house looks like in terms of layout and footprint. Before I wrap this chapter up, there is one thing I need to mention, and it's this: I would be careful around two and three story houses. Any time you offer a rental unit to the market, it makes good sense to open up your potential audience as much as possible.

Well, retirees don't want anything that's not on one level. Families with small children also usually prefer one level. Heck, I prefer one level! Not to mention the liability you open yourself up to when you consider the hazards that staircases present.

Stairs in your house-hack are simply not the best thing and should be avoided whenever possible, in my opinion.

Chapter 10

How Do I Hedge Regulatory Risk with House Hacking?

Introduction

To begin this particular discussion allow me to first remind you, yet again, of the three varieties of house-hack:

- a. Equity
- b. Cash Flow
- c. Blended

Before you say, "Oh no, here he goes again!" just bare with me one more time, as I think some of this imagery may clarify things a bit further.

<u>Winning Through Offense</u>

Equity house hacking is the winning-through-offense model. The focus is on creating equity. No attention is given to hedging the exit risk. No attention is given to anything resembling defense at all. Equity House Hacking is simply go - go - go.

<u>Winning Through Defense</u>

Cash Flow House Hacking is all about winning through defense. All attention is placed on the income, which offsets the cost of ownership, which accomplishes two things. One—it becomes possible to live an upscale lifestyle for less, and therefore with less risk. And two—it becomes possible to eliminate the exit risk, since the income lets us easily afford to stay put for as long as necessary.

Hedging One Against the Other, and Therefore Winning with Both!

I don't like to think in "either, or" terms. I prefer, whenever possible, to have all of the above. As this relates to my house hack, I want to focus on equity partially because this is what makes me rich, but also because equity can protect my exit should the income falter. And, of course, I also want to hedge my exit risk by having income, because if the equity is not there to exit as I planned, at least the income allows me to stay put for free or almost free. For this reason, I like the Blended House Hack model.

Never be a one-trick pony in anything you do!

Never leave yourself only one exit!

Vacation Rentals and Localities

Here's the thing, though. While the risk associated with equity is practically all market-driven, when it comes to the income in a house hack, it's not like it is risk-free. There are regulatory risks. The question is: since your winning formula depends on you being able to generate income, are there regulatory provisions, current or future, that may get in the way?

The answer is yes. Vacation rentals, specifically, are a heated subject at the government level in many municipalities.

In 2017, practically every major metropolitan area is or was struggling with how to deal with vacation rentals. The main beef of this model's critics is that vacation rentals are taking too many units out of circulation and thus creating a shortage of long-term rentals.

Something else critics like to say is that owners are turning their apartments into unofficial (read illegal) hotels.

It seems that every other week, I read sob-stories about how the landlord kicked out a long-term tenant who was paying $1,500 per month to convert the unit to a vacation rental that will earn $200 per night.

What those critics do not accentuate is that municipalities receive nice tax revenue from the hotel industry. Municipalities and the hotel industry have a codependent relationship, which neither party wants to disturb. And, unfortunately, in this context the short term vacation rentals are viewed as a threat.

But more importantly, something else that doesn't get enough play-time in the press is that for many people in highly desirable locations, home ownership is simply becoming unaffordable. For these folks the advent of websites like AirBnB and VRBO is indeed their saving grace. It's just a way to help pay the mortgage.

Yes, there are plenty of people pursuing vacation rentals as a business, and the argument around competition with the hotel industry certainly can be made. But, the way I see it, preventing a homeowner from renting out a room or part of his home as a vacation rental house hack to help out with the mortgage payment is just plain immoral. People are not asking for handouts; they are not asking for assistance to pay their debts. Instead, they are choosing to be entrepreneurial and bring a product to the market. This is what America is supposed to be about, yet some want to punish it?!

My family and I are living in our house for a mere $750 per month. But, in Chandler you can still buy a nice house for between $140 and $220 per square foot, meaning that a 2,000 square foot house will set you back $280,000 - $440,000. That's not cheap, but it's nothing compared to markets like San Francisco, Toronto, Boston, or Hawaii where a closet can cost $750,000. The ability to create vacation rental revenue can make the difference between being able to be a homeowner or not!

I would be remiss not to acknowledge that there is regulatory friction around all of this. That said, much like the smartphone a few short years back, websites like AirBnB, HomeAway, and VRBO have permeated our society to such an extent that it's difficult to imagine them disappearing.

Could there be additional regulations? Yes. Could there be added transactional costs in the future? Yes. But, even still, I think it is reasonable to assume that the vacation rental model will survive the current regulatory friction. For now we just have to cope.

The HOA

HOA stands for Homeowners Association. In any planned development, homeowners automatically become members of the HOA. Owners pay membership dues to the HOA, who is tasked with common-area upkeep.

Most of the nicer subdivisions across the country have HOAs, but in some states, such as Arizona, HOAs are more commonplace and more powerful than in others. The document which describes the rules and regulations that govern the HOA is called a CC&R (Codes, Covenants, and Restrictions).

An HOA's intended purpose is to keep the community from degrading by providing upkeep for the common areas and policing behavior of the owners. The HOA is there to maintain the look and the character of the neighborhood. To do so the HOAs use CC&Rs to itemize what can and cannot be done by the owners. Even in cases where state and local legislatures have settled the issue in favor of short-term rentals, the HOAs can still raise hell.

Now—here's the deal. The reality is that some HOAs are more willing to let things slide than others. In Arizona, there are HOAs that'll pitch a fit if you look at the sidewalk the wrong way. But, there are also those that let you live your life so long as you do not do anything that clearly contributes to deterioration of the neighborhood.

In Our Case

Once we were under contract to purchase our house, one of the first due-diligence items that we prioritized was the CC&R. Interestingly, I can tell you that, having looked at hundreds of properties in different neighborhoods, I'd only seen one CC&R in Chandler which didn't specifically address rentals with some sort of prohibitive language.

I am not telling you to go against HOA regulations as spelled out in the CC&R! However, if it becomes evident that everyone is doing something that you want to do, and the HOA is setting the precedent of looking the other way, would you go for it?

Here's How I Thought About my HOA

One: I am the second owner of this home. The previous owner built the house as an investment and placed a family member in it. From talking to the neighbors, I surmised that aside from this family member in the main house, there was someone else living in the Casita.

We are talking 10 years here—the HOA didn't care!

Two: After reading the CC&R, I drove the neighborhood for almost 3 weeks at different times of day. I was comparing what I'd read in the CC&R to what I actually saw out on the street. The subdivision looked very nice, but there were numerous instances of CC&R violations at virtually every house in the subdivision. This made us pretty comfortable that there was no strict adherence to the rules.

Don't misunderstand me, the HOA certainly didn't seem to neglect things. But, as I mentioned, some HOAs are more strict than others. In this case, they seemed "chill."

Three: Patrisha explained our intentions to rent out our casita to the listing agent and registered our concerns. The listing agent happened to know the property (and the neighborhood) from the very inception as she was the one who sold the house to the original owner. She corroborated our thinking relative to the HOA.

Patrisha and I, fully knowing that there are both macro and micro regulatory risks, felt comfortable that the potential upside of buying the home justified the risks. We knew we would be good neighbors. We certainly planned to improve the property. So, while there were risks, we moved forward.

How to Hedge Against Regulatory Risk

Analyze Risk / Reward

How do corporations deal with regulatory risk? Simple. If what they are doing cannot be construed as a federal offense, meaning nobody is going to jail over it, then the worst that can happen is either an order to cease and desist, or a fine, or both. So, corporations do what they need to do, figuring if they lose the court battle and have to stop, they'll stop. And in the meantime, just to be sure, they set up a slush fund so that if they do at some point have to pay a fine, the money is there.

Our house-hacking situation is very "small potatoes" but is no different. It is not a federal crime. We are not going to jail for doing a vacation rental house hack, which bothers absolutely none of the neighbors in any way at all. If we are asked to stop, we will try to negotiate; perhaps we'll offer to pay higher HOA fees. If that doesn't work, we may need to take the HOA to court, and considering that there is now statewide legislation in Arizona prohibiting discrimination against short-term rentals, we'd have a chance at prevailing:
Bill SB1350: http://www.azleg.gov/legtext/52leg/2r/bills/sb1350s.pdf

Interestingly, every lobbying group known to mankind supported this bill knowing that it will encourage a lot of revenue for everyone. But, there was one group that opposed it—American Hotel & Lodging Association...lol.

To Patrisha and I the risk-reward looked all right.

Do Your Research

If you know for a fact that a particular HOA is exceptionally difficult in this respect, are you going to buy a house hack there? Probably not, unless you are outwardly looking for a fight. If at all possible, buy in a pro-vacation-rental municipality. HOA's will do what they do, but if the state or city legislature has ruled in favor of vacation rentals, you at least have a case to make.

Hedge Your Risk with a Blended House Hack

Throughout the course of this book, I keep coming back to the notion that while I am all good with the emphasis in the house hack being placed on the income, there are a number of reasons why you need an equity component. Hedging regulatory risk is one reason. Your equity appreciation will hedge the income-loss risk, while your income will hedge the equity-loss risk. Buy something where you can win both ways, and then hopefully you'll at least win in one of these departments.

Conclusion

Sites like AirBnB and VRBO are fairly new, and the service they facilitate has created a bit of a shock to the system. However, in just a short time they have permeated our society beyond the point of critical mass whereby making them disappear will be very, very unlikely. Too many people are using these sites on both sides of the transaction in 2017.

There are risks in everything we do. There are choices that have to be made every day. I think that while you have to underwrite the possibility that the vacation rental house hacking model could still be shut down by regulators at whatever level, chances are that it's here to stay. I would wager that while it may become more highly taxed and regulated, it will not disappear.

Do the best you can to hedge yourself in all directions, and aside from research, the best way to hedge against regulatory risk is to do a Blended House Hack.

Chapter 11

How Do I Rehab my Vacation Rental House Hack for the Most Profit?

Step 1: Assess Your Competition

One of the most important lessons I've learned over the years is that while sometimes it's necessary to over-improve your product in order to be competitive in the marketplace, in other instances over-improving is not only unnecessary, but is downright dangerous. The impulse to be the best, to have things look the best, and to exhibit the most workmanship pride is very natural to all of us. But, we must learn to temper both the effort and the money we put into the project with the realities of what the marketplace is willing to pay. If you are not careful about this, it's easy to find yourself upside down on both equity and cash flow position in your project!

It's a fine line we walk to make things attractive enough to be highly competitive...but no more than that.

This begs the question: how exactly do you establish a budget and determine the extent of the work to do?

Let me paint you a picture.

When I get into my Tesla Model S to go to a destination I've never been to, the first thing I do is tell my car the destination address. Then, once I confirm that the car heard me correctly (can I just say here that my Tesla is much smarter than I...), the car plots the most appropriate course to the desired destination from the current location. To summarize:

A: I establish the destination.

B: The car notes the starting point.

C: The car formulates the best path forward.

The rehab process works the same way. Everything begins with understanding the marketplace. There is nothing more important than the marketplace. This is your destination. Understand—we can fix almost anything. But we obviously cannot fix the market!

So, the entire process is teed-up by understanding exactly what it will take to compete, which is a synergy of the product you bring to the marketplace and the price at which you will offer the product.

A: Assessing the Marketplace

In terms of my Casita project, I was dealing with a 234 square foot space. Competing with the hotels either on price or the size wasn't going to be difficult. The rooms in those hotels are not much bigger than what I offered. And as it relates to the pricing, anything remotely resembling a nice hotel room in Chandler runs at least $145 per night for a basic room without a kitchenette. Even if we had not installed the kitchenette, I was sure that it wasn't going to take much for our Casita to compete in that space, since I was prepared to be 60% less expensive.

On the other hand, a review of what was available through AirBnB and VRBO, which are the other dimension of the market, revealed that a person could book a 1-bedroom condo in a very decent location for around $85 per night. Such a condo would be more than twice the size of my Casita and include a full kitchen. Thus, while competing with hotels appeared to be a non-issue, vacation-rental competition was a concern.

Based on all of this, I could clearly see that I needed to end up with an outright A-Class space in terms of the finishing surfaces and amenities in order to compensate for the lack of space and to be competitive with the 1-bedroom condos.

So, having assessed the marketplace, this was the necessary outcome. Now let's take a closer look at what I had to work with exactly, and then I will walk you step-by-step through the entire process.

B: Assessing the Starting Point

First of all, a person can do a lot of things when remodeling a room; however, we cannot easily move load-bearing walls. That said, I was dealing with some real limitations within a 234 square foot space. While it really wasn't practical to try to make it any larger, I could certainly do lots of things to make it nicer and more functional. I could make my Casita nicer than most hotels—and even nicer than most of my vacation-rental competition.

The actual room was all right, though it was missing a ceiling fan. The bath, though, was a disaster (at least by vacation rental standards). The yellow-looking sink top looked dated, and was stained beyond possibility of repair. The tub had a basic, contractor-grade plastic surround. The nasty-looking wall cutout for soap and shampoo bottles—you could scrub that thing for a week straight and it would still be nasty. The fixtures were outdated and didn't function properly. And, of course, the toilet was broken!

So in essence, as far as high-end spaces go, this was a dump. Could I rent this on AirBnB with just a bit of elbow grease? Sure. But, would I be able to attract either the money or the quality of guests I wanted with this space in the condition it was in? Hell no. The only reason someone would be willing to book something like this for $30 per night is because $30 is all they've got!

This was not something that would interest the type of a person who is willing and able to spend $200 per night if necessary in order to get what they want but would take my Casita for $65 per night because nobody likes to overspend—that's who I wanted, and I knew I'd never attract them to this Casita as it was.

C: Plotting the Course

The remodeling scope-of-work options were as follows:

Option 1: Perform a good cleaning, replace the toilet, and put a little elbow grease into those plumbing fixtures. This would have been the least expensive way to go.

Option 2: Remove the closet door and tap into the bathroom plumbing to install a kitchen sink. I could opt for cheap cabinets and a formica countertop. And in the bath, I could put in a new Home Depot prefab marble sink-top, update the fixtures, and replace the toilet. This remodel would obviously be more expensive than option A, but it would give me an updated space with a kitchenette.

Option 3: Go for The WOW factor...

I kind of thought that in order to compensate for the size, I would have to go with Option 3—the wow factor. However, I certainly did not want to spend more money than the house could support relative to market valuation.

I relied on my wife, who is a realtor, to underwrite the equity side of this deal for me. Patrisha determined that an upgraded Casita that matched the upgrades in the main house would give our entire home the wow factor in the marketplace when we were ready to sell. We looked at the numbers together and figured we would, at the very least, double our cash investment on the resale value.

So, we went for the wow factor. Instead of simply removing just the closet door, we removed the door frame and the walls. This exposed some unfinished concrete slab floor. However, instead of just patching the tile, we created an attractive inlay threshold into the kitchenette. I know it doesn't seem like much, but wow factor is all about the details.

In the kitchenette, instead of basic Home Depot oak cabinets, we ordered upgraded maple cabinets with custom raised-panel doors and stain to match the bathroom sink-base and to keep the Casita finishes in line with the main house.

We laid a granite countertop with an under hung steel sink and installed an upgraded oil-rubbed bronze faucet. Though small, this kitchenette space turned out to be functional, clean, and classy.

In the bathroom, aside from replacing the toilet with something that wasn't going to clog every 20 minutes (I am not joking—this is important), we installed beautiful travertine tile in the tub surround all the way up to the ceiling to emphasize the high ceilings in the space.

We installed the same granite sink top here as we did in the kitchenette. People ask me how I chose the granite, and at the risk of sounding a bit redundant I'll tell you.

We bought our house as a Blended House Hack, which means resale value is important to us. The kitchen in the main house already had granite countertops, and Patrisha felt that it was important to match all of the bath sink tops and the kitchenette countertop to the countertops in the main kitchen. There is something *right* when things match!

Unfortunately for us, when matching new granite to something that was installed a decade ago, you don't just walk into Home Depot and ask pretty please. Just as with the cabinets for the kitchenette, we spent a bit more on the bathroom granite.

Step 2: Set Your Budget

What we were willing to spend fixing this Casita up was based on a few factors. First of all, as I discussed in the previous chapters, we simply needed to end up with a space that would be highly competitive in the vacation rental marketplace. And since the Casita was smaller than most units on AirBnB, we knew that we had to go the extra mile relative to the finishing surfaces.

Now—whenever doing any kind of remodel, as much as possible, we want to create more value than what we put in. We want to spend $1 to realize $2 on the resale. If you are not careful, you can easily spend too much and over-improve. It's not enough to make things very nice; we've got to create value!

As this relates to the rehab I did in the rest of the house, this was exactly the perspective I took. However, in the case of our Casita, the value was not so much in the equity my rehab would create (although obviously it did create some) as much as it was in the income I would generate. I needed to find a balance whereby the money I spent would create the most income in the most cost-effective manner. The income was going to recapitalize my investment, making it less necessary to worry so much about the equity in this case. But, I did have to peg things just right!

My general thinking went something like this:

Option 1: Perform a mid-range remodel.

- ❏ Remodel: $4,000
- ❏ Resulting Booking fee: $40 per night
- ❏ Resulting Avg. Occupancy Rate: 10 nights per month

$40/night x 10 Nights per Month = $400/Month

$4,000 investment / $400 per month of return = 10-month recapitalization time

So my theory here, based on my market research, was that spending less on the rehab ($4,000) was going to result in lower average annual occupancy and lower booking fees. And based on this, it would take 10 months to recapitalize my investment of $4,000.

Option 2: Go for The WOW factor...

- ❏ Remodel: $8,000
- ❏ Likely Booking fee: $65 per night
- ❏ Likely Avg. Occupancy Rate: 20 nights per month

At this rate, I'd be looking at average monthly income of $1,300 per month, which would recapitalize my investment for the remodel in about 6 months, which was roughly 4 months faster than option 1:

$65/night x 20 Nights/Month = $1,300/Month

$8,000 investment / $1,300 per month of return = 6.15-months recapitalization time

If I was right with my assumptions, Option 3 presented me with an opportunity to spend more but generate a disproportionately higher rate of cash-on-cash return, and in the process I'd create something much more attractive relative to the resale of the house, which would hopefully help my exit-equity position. This is a Blended House Hack, guys!

Incidentally, I must remind you here of one of the overriding concepts in this book, which is that tightening your belt in order to get ahead is not necessarily the right approach at all times. The above calculations prove this very point with the numbers. Spending more actually will yield a higher rate of return!

$4,000 investment recapitalized in 10 months is 120% annualized cash-on-cash return:

$400/month x 12 months = $4,800/annum

$4,800/return / $4,000 investment = 120% CCR

However, $8,000 recapitalized in 6 months is 195% annualized cash-on-cash return:

$1,300/month x 12 months = $15,600

$15,600/return / $8,000 investment = 195% CCR

What's better, 120% CCR or 195% CCR?

When we discussed down payments in an earlier chapter, I stressed my perspective that lower down payments are desirable because a down payment is akin to buying value, and we shouldn't be doing that. We should be creating value.

Well, this is a perfect case study of exactly that. Am I buying value by putting money into the rehab, or am I creating value? While making a larger down payment would have done exactly nothing to increase the value of my house as that relates to either income or equity, I think you can see that spending money on rehab definitely created value.

All of this may be a bit counter-intuitive for some of you. If so, go back and re-read this section. This is a book on house hacking, not real estate investing. And yet, a good house hack is the best investment you can make!

I spent $8,000 on the rehab all in.

<u>Enough With the Theory</u>

I have been at it for not quite 4 months as of this writing. In this time, our Casita has booked not quite $7,000. All things being equal, I feel comfortable telling you that we will make our projected annual cash flow of $15,000 - $16,000. Not only will that we double the amount we spent on remodeling the Casita, but if we keep at it, after two years we will completely recapitalize the entire house remodel!

Segue: I am now going to tell you that this morning, when I got up at 5 a.m., as I do every morning, our current guest had just left. He was in Chandler for 3 days for some type of sports boot camp.

I had a chance to talk with him. He is a business owner. He owns investment property in multiple states which includes both rental houses and acres of raw land in vacation destinations. He and I were able to speak at the same level about all things finance, and, in fact, I could learn from him.

He left the Casita spotless! I think he might have been the cleanest guest we ever had. He even took his garbage with him to the airport. I obviously still need to turn the unit, but this is going to be the easiest walk-in-the-park turn ever.

That's who we were able to attract to the Casita this time. Right before him, a young lady stayed with us who was here on consulting business, and her stay in our Casita was paid for by the corporation as part of their arrangement. Before her, we had a retired couple who stayed for eight days while they finalized with a builder all aspects of the home they are building for their retirement in Arizona.

There are a couple of things to note here: the last three guests are sort of indicative of a well-located, vacation rental house hack. We discussed this in an earlier chapter, but you want to choose a location people have lots of reasons to visit. Retirement, business, and sports event were all mentioned earlier as drivers of destination. Do you see?

The other important point is this—in all three cases, these people would have paid more. These folks were happy to get the highest quality for less money, but they had the capacity to spend more to attain that quality.

This is who I want in my house hack Casita: people who can afford $200 per night if that's what it takes to buy the quality they want, yet are happy paying $65 per night so long as they get the value. For them, it was quality first and pricing second—that's who I want staying in my Casita, 25 feet away from my family!

Step 3: Creating the Scope of Work

Scope of Work is what we call a document which outlines the parameters of a particular job, whether it's new construction or a rehab. While you'll get input from workers in the next step, at which time you will be free to amend the scope, I highly recommend that before you begin a project, you put your scope of work on paper to the best of your ability.

If you've never done this, don't be terrified. Just put as many things down as possible. Then, when walking through the project with contractors you'll be able to be very specific with them as to what you want done. And the contractors, in turn, will come back with detailed proposals.

<u>What to Include in the Scope of Work?</u>

I don't want to make this a book about rehabbing, because it's not. But, the devil is always in the details. The relatively obvious part of this is outlining all of the finishing elements. Finishing elements are all those things that you can see with your bare eyes. This includes things like drywall, paint, trim, door styles, countertops, sinks, lighting and plumbing fixtures, flooring, etc. In other words, every finishing texture that you can see with the naked eye has to be defined specifically. The best way to do this is just to simply specify the manufacturer's item numbers for everything you want. I mean *everything*!

Additionally, depending on how sophisticated you want to get, you discuss all of the things that you can't see because they are inside the wall. What kind of adhesives, screws, plumbing lines, etc... Be as specific as you can.

Also, the scope of work should reference timetables and completion dates, as well as what happens if things don't work out as planned. Are there penalties, and if so, what are they and how are they triggered? If inspections by the municipality are necessary, how does that work into the scope?

Finally, if the money needs to be disbursed in stages, what are the parameters?

Cost Overruns

The caveat to the scope of work is that as you go, you will almost undoubtedly make changes to the scope. For example, we changed a number of things mid stream. The tile we originally picked out for the master-shower base ended up being on back-order, and with time being of the essence, we chose to go with another product, which was more expensive in terms of the product itself and the installation.

Another additional cost for us was the glass enclosure for the master shower. Normally, shower enclosures are about 6-feet tall, and at first we thought this would work for us. But, once the guys ran travertine all the way up to that 9-foot-high ceiling, we realized that we needed a much bigger piece of glass. This meant that the glass needed to be thicker to maintain structural rigidity. It literally took 6 guys to carry that thing into the house.

Image G: Main Bathroom

Yep—the glass cost a bit more than we'd planned on, but boy does it look sexy! Don't you agree?

I am telling you this to drive home the point that there will indeed be cost overruns. Be prepared.

Step 4: Get Quotes for Scope of Work and Git 'R Done

I need to preface this section by telling you that, unequivocally, I paid too much when I paid $8,000. I don't feel bad about it at all, but it is the truth—I paid too much. I am not excusing myself, but let me explain.

First of all, I very obviously found myself in a city where I had done no business before, had no infrastructure in, and was unfamiliar with when it came to the finer points of everything from permitting to materials to workmanship. With time I would have sorted things out, but this brings me to the second point: I was definitely on a timeline.

We were, after all, living in an apartment. Once we gave notice to vacate, the fees to stay longer would have been substantial.

Additionally, the scope of work for the entire house was much greater than just this Casita. I was remodeling 2 baths, one of which (the master) was stripped down to the studs. Had it just been the Casita, perhaps I would have done things differently.

All said, I felt I couldn't take enough time to develop enough of an infrastructure to GC (general contract) my own rehab, which meant I needed to hire a general contractor. But, that's another mouth to feed, as they say, and as such I am sure I paid at least 20% more for everything across the board. In terms of the Casita, what cost me $8,000 should have cost $6,000.

This next part is Important!

The perspective that I want you to get comfy with is that you cannot use not being a local as an excuse. Neither can you use the argument that you are not a handy person and cannot fix things cheaply. Find a house hack with a good investment story and you should be able to source everything out!

Yes, you can't be a complete imbecile who isn't able to tell the difference between a rafter and a footer. Indeed, you have to develop some sense of what it takes, construction wise, to get things done. And yes, you must be logical and understand that hiring a contractor will cost money. But, given the right house hack you can still get this done!

And as it relates to finding a good contractor, the answer is two-fold:

One: Referrals are everything. Everyone I looked at for my house hack was referred to me by someone. A local friend and real estate investor referred a tile guy. The home inspector who did our pre-acquisition inspections referred a full-service contractor. Patrisha sold a home that had a really great remodeled bathroom; she got a referral to the contractor who did the work from the homeowner.

In short, I don't care how you get referrals, but unless you've got established infrastructure and know exactly whom you will use and for what, get referrals!

Two: Get multiple bids!

In my case, for example, the tile guy referred to me by my friend was able to give me the lowest quote on all of the tile work. However, that quote was just for the tile and did not include any plumbing, granite, drywall, and all of the rest of the work necessary to complete my projects.

I could have saved some money on the tile work by going with him. But, I chose not to. First of all, as I already mentioned, I did not want to GC all of the moving parts. I didn't know all of the players and wasn't comfortable taking the time to develop those relationships at a time when my family just needed some freaking showers to work.

More importantly, while his specific tile quote was the lowest, by the time I added my projections of the additional costs to get the scope of work accomplished, along with some cost overruns (which I was sure I'd run into if I were to try and GC this thing myself), the overall project savings just weren't worth the effort, time, and risk of delays.

The two other quotes I received were both higher than the first, but they were both from full-service general contractors. One of the companies specialized in high-end kitchen and bath remodels, and theirs was the highest quote. They were recommended by the inspector.

The other company specializes in insurance work, such as flood and fire restoration. They were the guys that did that bathroom in the house my wife sold. Their quote was about $7,000 lower than the highest one. That, and the fact that my wife saw their work and loved it, contributed to our decision to contract them.

All things considered, while I know I spent more than I could have, we were moved into the house on schedule, which was most important!

Chapter 12

How Do I Outfit My Vacation Rental for the Most Profit?

Making the Most of the Space

Now, I have to give credit to my wife here. I don't know if it comes through this way, but I'm not particularly patient. As soon as the remodel started, I began harassing Patrisha on a daily basis with questions about how the furniture was going to fit in the room, what furniture was going to go into the room, what I needed to buy to go into the room, etc.

Well, I think in the end we did pretty well. Based on our experience, here are the basics of what you want to consider.

<u>Furniture</u>

The overriding concept with furniture is: *clearly defined and functional spaces*. The spaces don't necessarily need to be large, but they need to be highly functional. The danger with small spaces, though, is that it's easy to cross the line from functional but small, to cramped. This was exactly what we were dealing with in a 234 square foot Casita.

At the very least, in order to feel comfortable, a room must accommodate a place to sleep, a place to sit, a place to eat, and a place to set the TV remote control, a book, and a pair of glasses by the bed. There needs to be a TV. There has to be a place for luggage, a place to store folded clothes, and a place to hang formal wear. There also needs to be a place for media and internet gear. A room (especially a small room) must get a lot of natural light, and yet there needs to be a way to keep the light out for when people want or need privacy and sleep.

This is what a decent room needs, and this was what we had to achieve in our Casita. How to achieve all of this within the confines of 234 square feet was totally beyond me, and I am happy that my wife stepped in.

We decided to reuse a queen size bed and two nightstands that we had no use for anymore. This was a really nice set that we brought with us from Ohio, but I wanted a king bed for myself, and I wasn't willing to settle, which rendered our fairly expensive, rustic-looking, cherry-stained oak bed frame with memory foam mattress useless. We also had two nightstands as part of this bedroom set.

We had also brought two flat-screen TVs with us, one of which we could spare. We also had a really nice comforter for the bed, enough spare dishes to outfit the kitchenette, and a few miscellaneous books to spare for the nightstands.

But that was all we had—everything else had to be bought.

Before I tell you how much it cost to outfit the 234 square foot Casita, let's ponder all that went in it.

Go Above and Beyond

<u>Our Shopping List</u>

- 4 large towels
- 4 hand towels
- 4 washcloths
- Towel rack
- Shower curtain
- Shower curtain rod
- Shower curtain rings
- Non-slip shower mat
- Bathroom rugs
- Tissue case
- Garbage can
- Blow dryer
- Microwave
- Mini fridge
- Keurig coffee maker
- Coffee caddy
- Silverware caddy
- Lamps for nightstands
- Coffee
- Creamer
- Kitchen garbage can
- Cutting board
- Knife

- Linens (two sets)
- Mattress pads (two)
- 2 king-size pillows
- 4 queen-size pillows
- Blackout curtains
- Chair
- Sheers
- Curtain rod
- Media cabinet
- Luggage racks
- Wall-mount clothes hanger
- Iron
- Ironing board
- Patio table and chairs
- Outdoor rug
- Potted decorative fake flowers
- Plants for the outside garden bed

That's a long list of stuff for a little Casita. But, since it is such a small space in comparison to what else is available on the market, we really needed to hit a home run relative to the amenities we were offering. It was important that we get it right. But it really wasn't cheap.

Before you laugh, let me tell you that the items on this list actually set me back about $2,000—stuff adds up when you want to go classy!

In the Kitchenette

We considered buying a used microwave and mini-fridge, but in the end decided against it because, for the best esthetics, I wanted the appliances to match. We got the look we wanted with stainless steel appliances from Target.

The Keurig coffee maker will set you back a few hundred dollars, but the alternative is a cheap Mr. Coffee, which will make a mess and—let's face it—won't make a decent cup of coffee. My wife is an avid coffee drinker, and she requires a really good cup first thing in the morning or she's just not happy. I knew that if our guests would be anything like her, a Keurig was a must. It's easy to clean and makes reliably good coffee every time. And again, a stainless-steel unit from Target did the trick.

We have no drawers in our kitchenette. There was barely enough width to install a sink-base cabinet while leaving room for the under-the-counter fridge. Obviously I couldn't put a drawer in the sink base. To cope with the lack of drawers, we did a couple of things.

We bought a matching Keurig coffee holder shaped like a rectangular drawer with 3 sections. We set it next to the Keurig, and this was enough to house all of the coffee accoutrements, leaving sparse countertop space for other things.

We also bought a counter organizer to hold a few forks and spoons. We made sure to add a corkscrew...everyone is a little happier after uncorking a bottle of red! Oh, yeah—did I mention we provide a bottle of red for all of our guests? Not everyone drinks the wine, but when you are going for 5-star, this kind of *over-the-top* thinking get's the job done!

Now, one thing that drives my wife and I crazy when we travel is that no rental kitchen is ever equipped with decent knives. You know—you go to cut something and just squash it instead. So, we bought a really good mid-size knife and a cutting board. This is a little thing that we think goes a long way.

In the cupboard, we stocked 4 short glasses, 2 wine glasses, 4 small plates, and 4 bowls. We used glass and china. No tacky (and toxic) plastic stuff!

As I mentioned, to go above and beyond guest's expectations we leave a bottle of red wine on the countertop. We also stock several assorted boxes of single-serving breakfast cereal and a box of muffins or fresh-made granola on the counter. And in the fridge, we stock 6 bottles of water, 2 small bottles of OJ, and 2 small bottles of milk. We do this for every guest. Some take advantage; others never touch a thing. But all guests appreciate the extra touch, which gets us great reviews on AirBnB and VRBO and keeps the guests comfortable for little to no expense on our part.

We also supply a bottle of dish soap, a roll of paper towels, and a brand new scrubber.

Finally, Patrisha adds a special touch with the kitchen towels. She folds three towels and ties them with a white ribbon. It's a small thing that takes her exactly 2 minutes to do, but the presentation is over-the-top, and the guests respond. We get comments like "Accommodations are superb!" and "Thank you so much for stocking some food!" And that's how you keep 'em coming!

In the Bathroom

While not small by any means, the Casita bathroom is not particularly large either. One of the best features in our house hack are the 9-foot ceilings, and they carry over to the Casita. When tiling showers, most people tend to only run tile about 7 feet up the wall. I don't understand this. Visually, running the tile all the way to the ceiling always helps the space feel more airy and grand. In our case, since we have 9-foot ceilings, the travertine really "pops." The extra cost was minimal, too.

The travertine tile on the walls, granite countertop with under hung sink, and oil-rubbed bronze fixtures contribute to a very classy feel. So— there's no clutter!

We spent the extra few bucks for a curved shower rod, which looks better from outside of the bathtub and feels better from within. Patrisha insisted that I install an oil-rubbed bronze space saver over the toilet. At first, I didn't think it was necessary, but it turned out beautifully and made a perfect place to store extra towels and washcloths.

And since there was no longer a need to store towels under the sink, we now had space for toilet paper, tissues, and cleaning supplies. Remember, we took out the closet to accommodate our kitchenette, but this meant that we had to find other places to stash certain household items that everyone needs.

Since our Casita is advertised specifically for no more than two guests, we provide 4 large towels, 4 hand towels, and 4 washcloths. The washcloths are important, so don't skimp. If you don't put them in, guests will ask...how do you think I know this? :)

I purchased a washable mat for inside the bathtub to avoid potential slipping. This didn't really have anything to do with aesthetics. It was more of a liability thing.

Lastly, we provide a high-end liquid hand soap for the sink. We do not provide any other toiletries.

The Bed

Ok, this is important. The bed has to be comfortable! If you think you can get away with a lumpy old mattress, you're mistaken. Your guests will talk about the bed, and if they can't get comfortable, they'll tell the world about it in their reviews. We've seen too many bad reviews of beds on AirBnB and VRBO, so we were willing to go the extra mile to make our guests as comfortable as possible.

In addition to the high-quality memory foam mattress, Patrisha decided to buy a good memory foam pillow top to boot. Also, if you're going for the *Above and Beyond* effect, I do recommend a solid bed frame. As I mentioned earlier, we had one, which was one place we were able to save some money. I highly recommend finding something solid!

As for the bedding, we purchased two mattress pad protectors, two sets of wrinkle-free sheets in two colors, two king-size pillows, and 4 queen-size pillows. Be sure to stay with wrinkle-free bedding, unless you want to spend hours ironing or spend ungodly amounts of money having it pressed.

The pillows are going to cost you $$$$ if you buy good ones. Patrisha bought good ones. I actually argued with my wife about this, but she knows quality, and she had a clear idea of the types of guests we would be getting. She reminded me about her and my parents and how none of them can get comfortable without a pillow here and a pillow there, etc., etc., etc. So, she won out, and we stocked the bed with 6 awesome pillows. This is another example of going above and beyond.

TV and Internet

Everyone wants internet and cable TV. Now, I can totally relate to the internet, seeing as I run internet businesses, but I haven't watched TV in a decade. But, whatever—people want it, so they got it.

We bought a very nice media cabinet with two deep drawers. It has a cherry finish that matches the bed frame. The TV rests on top, and this stand gave us some storage for guests' belongings.

The internet access point requires a bit of a lengthy explanation, but here it is.

I drive a Tesla, which is basically a computer on wheels. One of the defining characteristics of these cars is that they are capable of receiving OTA (over the air) updates. So, when I was shopping for a router, I chose a higher-end unit because I wanted to make sure that the WiFi signal would be nice and strong to reach the car in the garage.

Well, another benefit of a better router is that we are able to set up several accounts, which is exactly what we did. We set up password-protected guest WiFi for our Casita. I'll discuss this more in the next chapter.

Place to Sit and Watch TV

We bought a little padded chair at TJ Maxx which fit perfectly in the corner. It's a great place to sit and watch TV, or put your shoes on. It cost about $100, so that wasn't too bad.

Entrance / Daylight Exposure

Our Casita has a beautiful sliding door. It's oversized, and from inside the Casita it feels quite literally like almost the entire wall of the room is made of glass. While this is pretty and allows the room to stay well-lit during daytime hours, it's not that private, which needed to be addressed for everyone's sake.

I considered ordering vertical blinds, but because the doors are so wide and tall, I would have had to special order them. More importantly, Patrisha wanted to go a different aesthetic direction: she wanted a fancy curtain rod with sheers and blackout curtains. She felt completely committed to the notion that because we needed to do all that we could in order to compensate for the size, the curtain would add to the ambiance.

We had to order the curtains and sheers online to get the right size. She bought white sheers and neutral blackout curtains. I installed a double rod in the same oil-rubbed bronze finish as all of the other fixtures in the Casita. The sheers and curtains look great, though they were pricey. We paid about $450 all together for those.

That's quite a lot in my opinion, but what were the other options? Ordering vertical blinds would have cost about the same. Stock over-the-counter curtains would have looked silly dangling about 9 inches off the floor. In the end, you get what you pay for—these curtains do the job well and they look expensive because they are expensive!

Courtyard

There are two things everyone prefers in a rental if at all possible: a single level and some sort of outside space. This is just as true with regular rentals as it is with vacation rentals. And it's just as true with large 4-bedroom houses as it is with small apartments. But, obviously, when you are renting out a small space like our Casita, some sort of a dedicated outside space which your guests could have access to is an absolute must, in my opinion.

As I discussed in an earlier chapter, our house is shaped like a horseshoe which is fantastic also in that this footprint creates a natural courtyard. This space is not visible from the street, which allows for some very quaint landscaping possibilities.

Once a guest enters the premises through the gate at the street, they find themselves inside of this horseshoe courtyard. Our house has a nice enough curb appeal. But, we felt like this courtyard offered us a brilliant opportunity to take it over the top before the guest actually sets foot inside the Casita.

But, aside for the esthetics the courtyard serves a purpose. One of the clearly defined areas in any dwelling needs to obviously be a place to eat, with table, chairs, etc. Well, we could only do what we could do inside of our 234 square feet, and we just didn't have room for a table. But, remember—we are in Arizona, where life is easy and the weather is always great! So, Patrisha had me pick up a cast-iron table and two chairs at Target. This seating area actually accomplishes three objectives at once.

On one hand, it extends the Casita living space beyond the 4 walls and into the outdoors. In Arizona this is a very viable place to plant yourself with a laptop, cup of coffee, a snack, or a book. Indeed, every single guest we've hosted thus far has made use of this space.

Equally importantly, this seating area creates a point of separation between the main house and the Casita, making it feel like there is more linear footage between us than there actually is. This adds to the guests' sense of privacy.

And finally, this little sitting area is like a tiny island in neutral waters. When I see my guests at this table, I open the door and ask them if there's anything I can help with. Small gestures like that are the difference between an AirBnB vacation rental and a hotel. And more often than not, things progress into a conversation, which leads to some sort of a relationship. And that results in 5-star ratings. This little table with two chairs comes in very handy indeed!

<u>Space and Storage</u>

This was one of two obvious omissions on our part in the beginning. As I mentioned, a chest-of-drawers that the TV sits on serves as clothes storage. It has two very deep drawers, and that's certainly enough to accommodate anyone for a week or two.

The thing we missed, though, is that some clothes need to be hung. There was a time in my life when I spent my days on stage, in a tux, with a fiddle in my hands. A place to hang formal wear would not have escaped my attention back then. Alas, I've been wearing shorts and tee-shirts for so long that I totally blanked on this. Case in point was the second group we ever hosted. A couple came to Chandler for a wedding. Obviously, formal attire needs to be hung. Duh...

You know, it actually wasn't the easiest thing to figure out a clothes hanger. A typical hanger bar protrudes about 16 inches away from the wall to accommodate the hangers. I couldn't do that. As small as the Casita is, I just could not spare room. Looking for a more elegant solution, I went to Lowes, Home Depot, and looked online. I just couldn't find anything that would fit the bill.

And then, we happened to be at Target and there it was—a wire swivel hanger for less than $10. For all of the fancy and expensive pieces I'd seen, this thing is brilliant in its simplicity. What you can't see in the picture is that, at the top, it actually has a loop for hanging on top of a door. However, this loop can easily be broken off, making it possible to install this thing flush on the wall.

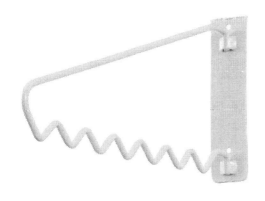

What's the best thing about this? You hardly notice it if it's hung high enough and out of the way. Plus, since it swivels, it can close completely flush with the wall. And with this, we were able to accommodate a place to hang clothes for less than $10, totally out of the way, and with just 2 anchors and screws.

It's always the little things that create the most headaches and provide the best solutions.

<u>Laundry Services</u>

We do not offer laundry services at our Casita. However, about two months into our vacation rental house hack, we welcomed a guest who happened to be in the midst of a job transfer. His position required suit-and-tie attire every day.

I am sure that we should have thought of this, but when he asked whether an iron and an ironing board were provided, both Patrisha and I exclaimed—duh!

Needles to say, I ran out and bought both. The ironing board folded and slid underneath the bed, and the iron went under the sink.

Conclusion

There are three concepts I want you to remember relative to outfitting any space.

One: Staging is there to soften the negative effects of physical shortcomings which cannot be easily remedied. In our case, size was the issue, so we looked for ways to overcome it.

Two: You must create a highly usable space. It doesn't have to be large. But, it does have to be very comfortable.

Three: WOW factor. Little things matter!

Have fun with it! :)

Chapter 13

How Do I Market My Vacation Rental for the Most Profit?

Introduction

I need you to understand something. As of this writing, I've only owned my house hack for about 6 months. I made a very quick decision to write this book because I see such tremendous power in the house-hacking strategy, and I wanted to deliver this information to you ASAP.

In this chapter, I will tell you everything I do to market my vacation rental. But, to the extent that I only have this one vacation rental, and I've only been at it for about 6 months, I do not pretend to be an absolute, all-knowing authority on marketing vacation rentals.

With that said, the marketing process is super easy, at least on a small scale such as what we are discussing here. The entire funnel is automated, and while it will require some input from you, most of the process is super simple. Here we go.

The #1 Key to Marketing a Vacation Rental

I am getting ahead of myself a bit, but I really need to drill this into your consciousness. Understand—a vacation is not a necessity in anyone's life. A vacation is something we do if we can afford it. A vacation rental, therefore, is a choice item. And as is the case with any other choice item, we are appealing to people who have some extra money to spend.

Guess what: people who have money to spend tend to know exactly what they want, and they don't like to compromise!

The essence of the entire conversation we had in the previous chapter, detailing our perspective on every aspect of how I remodeled our Casita, boils down to presenting an image which would be appealing to people who know what they want and have some money with which to pay for it. And how do we deliver this image?

Pictures!

Your Pictures Will Make Or Break Your Rental!

When you've got your rental together, your next job is to get great pictures. Since we are talking about vacation rentals, your guests are not going to be local. They can't simply hop into the car and drive by. They can't schedule a viewing appointment. Instead, your prospective guests will be viewing your property on the internet and comparing the pictures to those of your competition. This entire process, all the way through booking, will take place on the internet.

The first opportunity you get to make a good first impression, therefore, is with your presentation on the internet. And while there are other important elements, the pictures you post are absolutely crucial to staying booked and making money!

What this inevitably means is that it doesn't matter how good of a rehab you've done if your pictures suck, which brings me to my next point. Some of you think you are all kinds of artistic with your iPhone camera...NO! If you are adept at taking photos, and have truly good equipment, go for it and see how things look. Personally, I opted to pay a professional. It cost me $80 to get a professional photographer, and I am convinced this was the right thing to do.

A professional photographer will get the right angles. They will make sure the lighting is good. They will Photoshop out the reflections in the bathroom mirror. Don't underestimate the importance of this initial investment in your asset.

Now, let me paint *you* a picture.

There is a line from a favorite movie of mine. The movie is called *Hitch*, starring Will Smith, Kevin James, and Eva Longoria. This is a really great romantic flick in which Will Smith's character is a consultant who helps regular guys overcome their fears and self-limitations in order to approach and win the hearts and affection of their dream girl. Kevin James' character is a clumsy, overweight, yet lovable and endearing accountant who works at a firm representing a New York City socialite. He falls madly in love with the socialite, yet she knows nothing of his existence. So, he hires the consultant to help...the whole setting is rather comical.

My favorite line, though, is in the very beginning of the movie. While describing the objective of the first date to a client, Will Smith's character says:

Your job is not to make her like you.

Remember, she already said yes, when she could have said no.

She made plans with you, when she could have just blown you off.

Your job is not to screw it up!

In other words, after you get those kickass photos, your place really needs to look like the pictures that you posted online, or your reviewers will hang you out to dry!

Which Picture Should I Pick for the Cover?

When your listing appears on the marketing platforms, there will be one photo that is showcased. It'll be a small thumbnail-sized image on the listing scroll, and once someone clicks on the listing, this picture will maximize, with the remaining photos displayed as thumbnails below or to the side.

Obviously it's important to get noticed among hundreds of listings someone might scroll through, and it's this one picture that should help do the trick. It's important to pick the right photo for the cover.

Personally, as I thought about this, I had trouble picking out one photo. I mean, the kitchenette was great, with those sexy cabinets and granite countertop. The travertine in the shower was fantastic as well. But, how do you lead with a kitchenette when you are competing against 1-bedroom units with full kitchens. I may have a granite countertop while they don't, but what they do have are full kitchens, and mine has a base unit and 2 uppers. Do I really want to push this image?! And how do you lead with a picture of a bathroom. Yeah it's really nice, but it's a freaking bathroom; so what if it makes you feel like the king of the hill.

Bottom line, I had trouble knowing which image to use here. So, I took this down to the lowest common denominator in my thinking.

When selling anything, the most important thing you can do is to counter and disarm the biggest objections. In other words, when looking at your unit through the eyes of potential guests, what is the single biggest weakness that people are liable to note? I decided to opt for the cover photo which did the best job of nullifying that weakness.

For us, size was the ultimate concern. We knew this going in, and it was reasonable to assume that this would be a concern for the potential guests as well. Obviously we did all that we could to address this with quality finishing textures and staging, as discussed previously. But the image we decided to use for our cover was the one which we thought created the most perception of depth and space:

Image H: Casita interior 2

Marketing Platforms

I am sure that the pros who run multiple vacation rental units in multiple destinations will tell you that there are about 30 marketing platforms that you have to use. And, they will also tell you to use services which syndicate all of those platforms, schedulers, etc. For my money, with this house-hack vacation rental, there are only three big boys: AirBnB, HomeAway, and VRBO. And since HomeAway now owns VRBO, which means that all of the listings on one site are automatically included on the other, I only see a need to be on two marketing platforms. I chose AirBnB and VRBO.

<u>Setting Up Your Account</u>

Before you can actually list your house hack for rent, you will need to create a host account. Both platforms will want to know that you are who you say you are and that the property you are listing is truly yours.

There are a lot of scammers out there! Before we dig into some of the property-specific questions, allow me to mention a few points relative to your profile.

Photo: As part of completing your profile, you will be asked to upload a photo of yourself. Not that you need a suit and tie for this, but please refrain from anything that captures you either drunk, naked, or stoned. I get that you are a fun person and great company, but understand—potential guests are more suspicious of you than you are of them. Everyone is concerned with being scammed.

You get my point? Just don't overdo the personality. Consider which photo you use carefully...it tells a story on its own. You want to appear "real." You want to be seen as just a homeowner willing to share a space that you've put effort into making very nice. You are that entrepreneurial individual or couple who realizes that, with this income, you can pay your mortgage.

This "real" persona is relatable and is indeed the most powerful competitive advantage against the pros. After all, if your guests wanted a corporate environment, they'd have rented a hotel room. So, the fact that they are looking at your ad just means that you need to not mess up a good thing!

Other Info: The platforms will ask you all kinds of information, everything from your birth date to your telephone number to your emergency contact. Some of this is required because they want to verify that you are who you say you are.

Getting Paid: The other aspect of your host profile that I'd like to mention is how you get paid for hosting. I won't bother outlining the exact workflow of setting this up, because things change often with these sites. But, you'll need to submit account information for direct deposit. This is how both AirBnB and VRBO will pay you for hosting.

Keep in mind that the first payment may take a little longer, at least it did in my case. However, once you are in their system, you should get paid within 48 hours of your guests' arrival.

Property Listing Profile

Once your host profile is ready to roll, you'll be able to proceed to the property profile. Both platforms will take you through a rather long list of fields whereby you can pick and choose anything that applies to your unit, from size to HVAC type. Not all of this is crucial, so just do the best that you can. Below, however, are some of the more crucial aspects of your property profile:

Description: As part of completing your property profile, you will have an opportunity to write a short paragraph to describe your vacation rental, the main attributes, amenities, local attractions, etc. Everything we are doing in this property profile is to get our unit to be noticed among dozens and hundreds of the available listings in your marketplace. Aside from your photos, this little property description is your best chance to help your property stand out. And it's important not only because of what it says, but how it says it.

Understand something: the person reading your description is pre-conditioned not to trust you. This person is unlikely to be a regular repeat user of these sites. It might be their first time. It might be their third time. But, they are still in a psychological state whereby they wonder if taking the chance on your rental is worth the savings against simply staying at the Marriott Hotel.

You've got to sell your unit! And to make things just a bit more challenging, you are only allotted so many characters in the field. :)

Here's how mine reads:

Beautiful Casita with kitchenette, granite counter tops and travertine tile in the bath. Near restaurants, shopping, and a movie theater. Minutes from 202 and I-10. 12 min from Intel and Price Corridor, 30 min from Sky Harbor, and 3 min from Chandler Municipal Airport. Private entry and sitting area in a private courtyard. Pool access Mar - Oct. Memory foam queen bed. WiFi and cable TV. Good for couples, solo adventurers, and business travelers. Electric car charger avail for a fee.

There's lots of ground to cover in a little bit of space. There are lots of concerns to alleviate. What we focused on is providing answers to the most commonly asked questions:

- ❏ Is there a private entry?
- ❏ Is there an outside area?
- ❏ Is there WiFi and TV?
- ❏ How close is it to shopping and transportation?
- ❏ How close is it to major employment centers?
- ❏ How close is it to major freeways?

And aside from answering those questions, we simply tried to paint an image of a classy place. What do you think—have we succeeded? Based on who we attract, I'd say we did well.

Frequency: One of the questions you'll need to answer is how often you want to host someone in your rental. Patrisha and I, for obvious reasons, chose the "as often as possible" option, but obviously you don't have to.

Minimum Stay: Minimum stay refers to the minimum number of nights you will allow per booking. While you can indicate that you allow 1-night bookings, we chose a 3-night minimum. The reasons are several:

One—we did not feel comfortable with the sheer volume of traffic which would result from people coming and going every single day. We did not want the extra attention.

Two—we did not want to be turning the unit every day. This is simply not cost-effective considering our nightly rates in Chandler. If I could charge $300 per night, perhaps I'd reconsider. But at $65 per night, it makes no sense.

House-rules: The way to ensure that your ad gets noticed by the right people is to create a detailed description of what is involved and who is welcome. This section is called *House Rules,* and it is displayed for everyone to see right on the front of the your ad.

For example, we don't want any more than 2 people in our Casita. There is only a queen-size bed in there which can accommodate no more than 2 people, and we did not want any improvisation around this. The space is designed to be used by 2 people—period. I think it's important that people know this upfront so nobody wastes anybody's time.

Additionally, we don't want people under the age of 25. I remember myself at 22, and my 22-year-old self is not what I want in my Casita.

Also, we don't want to host smokers. Not only is the second-hand smoke bad for people, but it is terrible for the property. The smell permeates drywall and every soft surface.

We also do not want to deal with pets. Pets are just a messy thing. Cat hair, dog hair, accidents in the room: the list goes on. No pets.

We put all of these guidelines in the *House Rules Section*, which is displayed right on the front page of your listing where everyone can see. And you know—people read these!

Finally, I should put the house rules in perspective. Understand that your profile photo, photos of your rental, description of your rental, and now the house rules: all of these are snapshots that speak to who you are and what you're all about. You are using these different tidbits of information to paint whatever picture of yourself that you want.

The fact that you clearly display an age restriction says something about how you roll in life, and so does the fact that you have a no-smoking policy and that you don't allow pets. Will this lose you some guests? Yes. Will you turn some people off? Absolutely. But, this works in both directions.

So, the first thing you need to do is determine whom you want to attract, then work backwards with your presentation.

Cancellation: You'll be asked to state your cancellation policy, which will be displayed publically as well. Below is a screenshot of our policy:

Owner's cancellation policy:

50% refund for cancellations more than 14 days before check-in date.

100% refund for cancellations more than 30 days before check-in date.

Pretty standard. See what others are doing and model yours after that.

Service Agreement: Think of the service agreement for vacation rentals as the equivalent of a lease for a long-term rental. This needs to be a comprehensive document outlining every piece of minutiae you can think of.

Essentially, the main purpose of the service agreement is to protect you from liability as much as possible. Conveniently, both AirBnB and VRBO provide a way for you to insert this into the booking workflow so that the very act of booking your unit attests to the guest agreeing with and accepting the policies set forth in your service agreement. Consult your attorney on this.

Pricing: On both sites, you can set the following pricing aspects:

- Nightly rate
- Weekend rate (if different)
- Weekly
- Monthly
- Event pricing

All of these are self explanatory. The main difference is that as of this writing on AirBnB you can select a range of minimum and maximum nightly rates. Also, AirBnB offers a feature they call *smart pricing*. The price range you set combined with smart pricing will allow AirBnB to select the optimum price for your unit at any given time based on their algorithm, which takes into account competition, seasonality, events, and other factors.

187

While I am sure that the pros find this feature quite helpful, I haven't seen too much benefit thus far. Good old fashion, real-time competition research is still the name of the game for me. If I have a vacancy, I take it upon myself to study the other available listings and adjust my pricing accordingly. This might sound daunting to you, but with one unit it really is not.

There is one thing that you need to keep in mind regarding booking rates. While you can see the rates the competition is advertising, you need to realize that these may or may not be the actual agreed-upon rates. There are a couple of things to note here.

As part of the booking process, owners can offer discounts. And even if no discount is advertised, guests can ask for discounts, in which case it's entirely up to the owner whether or not to accommodate.

The thing is, though, if any negotiation takes place, it is not public knowledge. Thus, while you can see the advertised booking rates, the rate doesn't necessarily reflect the actual market conditions.

It can be somewhat of a challenge to underwrite the market booking rates. Do the best you can.

Fees: Both AirBnB and VRBO are pretty good about allowing you to charge whatever fees your particular vacation rental warrants. For example, the most commonly charged fee is a cleaning fee. As you scroll through the listings on these platforms, you'll notice that most of the owners charge anywhere from $25 to $50. This is a one-time fee that is assessed on a per-booking basis.

However, your particular property may warrant other fees. For instance, if you have a boat dock, you may require a docking fee. If you want to provide laundry services, you can charge for that. Patrisha and I, for example, offer electric-car charging for a fee since we drive a Tesla and our house is wired.

Occupancy Taxes and Transactional Fees: Most States and municipalities require some sort of occupancy tax. This tax is actually levied on the owner of the property, but most of the time it is passed along to the guest or tenant. The next time you stay in a hotel, look at your bill—you'll see an occupancy tax.

It falls upon you to determine how much, if any, to collect. So—do some research.

Payment Options: Both platforms allow you to accept partial payments. Don't. All moneys should be collected by the platform in full at booking time. Done!

Service Fee: Both platforms charge service fees. Think of these as transactional fees. This is how they make their cut. Furthermore, they charge both the host and the guest.

These are subject to change, so I don't want to spend much time on this. However, below are screenshots from both websites discussing their policy as of 2017.

AirBnB

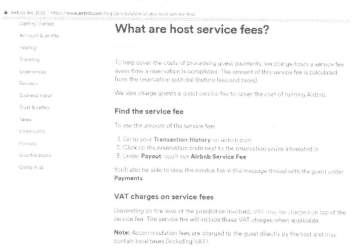

VRBO

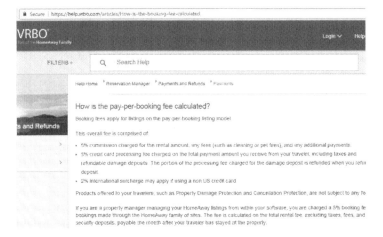

I can tell you that in my own experience, AirBnB ends up being less costly.

Managing the Calendars

Each of the platforms maintains a calendar. When a guest books your place, this automatically posts to the calendar, so everyone can see that the unit is now unavailable. It's very simple indeed; this requires no input from you.

However, since we are using 2 platforms, and since there is no synchronization between these platforms, it's necessary to manually ensure that the calendars on both platforms match so as to avoid double bookings. So, when someone books on AirBnB, you must immediately (or as soon as possible) reflect the booked dates on VRBO, and vise versa.

Now, there are service providers out there who can synchronize all of the listing sites for you. However, considering the cost, which is not cheap, I didn't do it for just one unit. If I had 5-10 vacation rentals booking at the same time, then I'd likely be using such a service.

Finally, hosts are free to take units off-line any time. If your family is coming to visit, or if you are going on vacation and are not comfortable letting guests in while you're gone, simply block the dates as unavailable on both calendars. It's easy.

Instant Booking

In the booking settings on both AirBnB and VRBO, the owners are given the option to either accept instant bookings or require prior contact and approval from the owner. I like instant booking because if someone wants to lie to me, the fact that I am talking to them will not change this. And, unfortunately, there's very little recourse for me. If there is a weakness to this model, it's in the fact that we do not materially participate in the guest-qualifying process.

Smartphone Apps

Even if you choose to allow instant booking, some guests will have questions about the property prior to pulling the trigger. Something to note here is that both AirBnB and VRBO track your response rate and time and incorporate this data into their rating of you as a host.

Thus, the faster you can respond, the better. And it's really helpful that both platforms offer smartphone apps which allow for a full range of services to help you conduct business. The most useful element, though, is being able to respond to inquiries on the go.

Personally, I think that the AirBnB app is a bit more polished. But, both apps work fine.

Screening Your Guests

Arguably, the single biggest risk in the vacation rental business resides in the fact that there is precious little we can do to screen guests. Yes, the platforms do require a completion of the guest profile, and they do their best to verify the provided information. Yes, as owners we can check guest profiles, and look over the reviews of the guest posted by other owners. But, at the end of the day, unlike with a long-term rental applicant, we are not pulling the guest's background and credit history, nor are we verifying income and duration of employment. This is indeed a bit of a *cat-in-the-bag* situation, which definitely presents some risk.

However, the simple reality is that if you want to make more cash flow, chances are you will need to go the vacation rental route. And everything we've discussed so far in this book; from the optimum footprint of your house hack; to the type of remodel you do; to the staging; to your house rules; to your marketing materials: to your pricing; all of this was geared to hopefully attract the best qualified guests.

We are throwing caution to the wind in some sense, and anything we can do to steer this ship in the right direction is important!

Reviews!

We live and die by the reviews guests leave on the platforms. There is just very little I can add to that. Getting as many reviews as possible, as quickly as possible, is imperative. Both AirBnB and VRBO help you with this because they prompt guests to review your unit. But, you should also reach out whenever possible.

Finally, you should understand that you may have to discount your unit until you have plenty of reviews. No matter how nice your pictures look, it is hard to be the new kid on the block next to a unit that's been there for 18 months and has 16 five-star reviews.

Conclusion

At the end of the day, marketing a vacation rental is infinitely easier than many other aspects of real estate investing. The advent of sites like AirBnB and VRBO, which centralize and streamline the entire process, take a lot of the busy work off of your plate. By the way, this is yet another advantage of vacation rentals as opposed to a long-term rental, so consider that when choosing your house hack.

Well, the only thing left to discuss before setting you loose is the actual management of the physical asset. How do you let guests in? How do you turn the unit between the guests? What's involved with managing the business end of your house hack?

It's actually rather easy. Keep reading.

Chapter 14

How Do I Turn a Vacation Rental Between Guests?

Introduction

If there was one item which concerned me most prior to getting into our house hack, it was the extent of the time commitment I was signing up for. While I know lots of things about real estate and rentals, I'd never done anything with vacation rentals until now.

Having researched the market and having underwritten the nightly rates and their cyclicity, I realized that we were going to have to do the best that we could to stay more or less full all of the time in order to create enough revenue to really make this house hack worthwhile. Let me put this differently: while I would have gratefully accepted income of $500 per month if that was all I could get, I really wanted more...much more. And I thought I could get it, but we would have to stay full!

The very reason to pursue vacation rentals as opposed to long-term rentals resided in the calculation that, due to the higher velocity of money, we'd be able to generate much higher revenues. But, if we were going to have guests one after another (hence high velocity of money), my time commitment relating to management and turns was the obvious trade-off, and I must admit—it was a concern.

As it turned out, however, the turns are not an issue at all for me. In fact, considering that a typical day for me involves dropping the kids off at school, followed by a workout, followed by either a lounge chair in front of the pool or a very comfortable leather armchair in the living room with my laptop and cell-phone, I don't see any reason to outsource the turns...period.

Turns are easy. They take 50 minutes. And handling turns myself definitely represents a competitive advantage. Plus, I'm proud of my little Casita, and I feel a strange sense of pride in its presentation. Come to think of it, it's similar to the pride I take in cleaning my Tesla Model S. :)

How Much Time Do I Spend on Turns?

In a typical month, we host anywhere between 4 and 6 parties. Between guests, my time-commitment turning the Casita can be broken down into primary time commitment and secondary time commitment. The primary time is the time I actually spend inside of the Casita cleaning and getting it rent-ready for the next guest. The secondary time commitment comes from the fact that the washing machine, drying machine, and dishwasher take whatever time they take, and I can only do so much to make the machines go faster. I've tried pleading, rationalizing, and even threatening, but the machines just do what they were designed to do...lol.

I've got my system down to where my primary time commitment is about 50 minutes per turn. This means that if we had 6 parties stay with us throughout the month, my primary time commitment would total no more than 6 hours. Most months it's closer to 4 hours.

And yes, on an intellectual level, I do hate trading hours for dollars, and I do try to avoid it as much as possible. The argument goes like this: if I were to pay someone $15 per hour to do these turns, my monthly cost would be $90 or less. Certainly, I could occupy my time doing something that generates much more revenue than $90. Such is the intellectual premise, right?

Practically, though, turns are time sensitive. With 6 parties coming in and out in one month, one guest is often leaving at 11:00 a.m. and the next is showing up at 4:00 p.m. And they often request to check in at noon, or something close to that. With this in mind, the cleaning service would have to be very much on-call and willing to be very flexible. This costs much more than $15 per hour!

So, if we consider this Casita my job (something whereby I trade time for money), then in a month requiring 6 turns, 6 hours of my time facilitates a minimum of $1,600 of revenue. Therefore, we could say that I am getting paid $266 per hour:

$$\$1,600 / 6 = \$266$$

And in a month when the Casita only makes half as much income, it's because only half as many guests visited, which requires half as much time commitment for the turns. So, if you want to look at the notion of not outsourcing these turns as a job for me, then we kind of know my hourly pay: $250 per hour...or more.

Guys—I am blessed in that I don't have a real job. My time is quite flexible. The turns are so easy. As far as trading hours for dollars, I can think of worse ways. I just do the turns myself, at least for now. Perhaps I am wrong in taking this approach, and if you disagree, you can source the turns out.

Now, the secondary time commitment absorbs about 2 more hours per turn. I have to wait on the machines to run through their cycles. But, since all I am doing in this case is waiting, which means that I can be productive in some other way, I don't think that this time is worth another mention.

And now let's take a look at what turning our unit actually looks like. Let's start from the end. The guest has checked out. I have the key. What are the steps involved with getting the Casita rent ready?

Checkout

In the Casita, we have a nice little handbook called *Guest Handbook*, which you can find at **www.JustAskBenWhy.com/househack**. One of the sections in the guest handbook discusses the checkout procedure. Among other things, we inform the guests that our check-out is at 11:00 a.m., and we make it clear that at exactly 11:01 a.m., we are coming in to turn the unit. We have never had an issue with someone not complying.

The night before a guest checks out, I post the *Checkout Checklist* on the door (you can download it at **www.JustAskBenWhy.com/househack**). This is the same information that is covered in the guest handbook, but there is a reason I post it. The checkout checklist is a simple one-page document, and at the bottom of the page there is room for a personal, handwritten note from me. Not only does this allow me to manufacture a good last-communication experience with my guests, but it is also a great opportunity to remind them to leave us a good review. I am of the opinion that if you want something in life, you ask for it. Considering the importance of these reviews to the business model, I just ask for a good one!

Also, the night before guests check out, I place the lockbox on the front gate. On their way out, the guest leaves the key in the lockbox for me to pick up. I will speak more about the lock situation later on when we discuss the check-in process.

Once the guests are out and I have the key, the turn begins.

The Turn

Below is the list of tasks I perform in the order I perform them.

1 - Clean-out: I strip the bed. I carry all of the sheets, bath towels, kitchen towels, and bath rugs to the laundry room in the main house. This is definitely a workout since it requires me to take exactly 27 steps (I've counted). I am earning my pay, for sure!

Washing all of these items usually requires 3 loads of laundry. We start the first wash cycle immediately. By the time the first load is ready to go into the dryer, I'll be done with the entire turn and on to writing my next book, or something...

On my way back to the Casita, I grab all of the cleaning supplies.

2 - Dishes: For our guest's convenience, we stock a few glasses, dishes, cups, and utensils in the kitchenette. I collect all of these, even if they look like they haven't been used, and walk across the courtyard for the second time to start the dishwasher.

On my way back to the Casita, I grab a fresh set of linens.

3 - Make Bed: We have two sets of sheets for the bed. We also have two comforters, as well as two mattress protectors. With a clean bedding set ready to go, making the bed is a 10-minute proposition.

From here, I move onto the actual cleaning.

4 - Clean: The toilet, shower, bathroom counter, and kitchen counter all need cleaning and disinfecting. The mirrors need to be cleaned, and sometimes the windows as well. The fridge and microwave in the kitchenette need to be wiped down. At this time, I also make sure to restock paper towels in the kitchenette and the toilet paper, tissues, and hand soap in the bath.

This step is the largest time commitment for me,

occupying about 30 minutes for everything.

5- Kitchenette: For our guests' convenience, we provide a Keurig coffee machine in the kitchenette. It needs to be cleaned. We also provide an assortment of cereal, coffee, and items in the refrigerator, such as some milk, OJ, and water. Finally, we stock the kitchenette with a bottle of wine and a fresh box of granola bars or muffins.

Not everyone takes advantage of these items, so not every item needs to be replaced during each turn. However, this does require a trip to the store, if for nothing more than the fresh treats. My wife is a realtor, so she is out and about all day every day (in my Tesla, I might add). So once the guests leave, she takes an inventory of the items in need of restocking and buys them while she's out.

Would it be the end of the world if we didn't go through the trouble of providing a few things for people? No. But remember, we are shooting for the WOW factor!

6 - Vacuum: How long do you think it takes me to vacuum 234 square feet? Yep, about as long as it takes to walk the 27 steps from the Casita to the laundry room, haha. I also like to dust the bed frame, night stands, media cabinet, and TV with microfiber cloths and beeswax polish. It makes everything look extra clean, and it smells good.

7 - Restock Clean Dishes and Pantry Items.

8 - Restock Clean Towels and Bath Mats.

9 - Prepare the Lockbox.

That's all: nine steps which occupy about 50 minutes of my primary time commitment. I was initially concerned about the time commitment. There is no reason to be concerned. This is easy!

Check-In

My system for guest check-in is pretty simple. Prior to their arrival, the guest receives a message from me on AirBnB or VRBO with check-in instructions. This is the exact message I send out (I have it memorized in my Google drive and only change names and lock combinations):

Hi, _____ - we are looking forward to hosting you soon at the Tuscan Inspired Casita in beautiful Chandler!

A few instructions:

Our address is: _____

As you pull up to the house, you will see steps leading to a gate. Park your car on the street right in front of the steps. On the gate (bottom left) you will find a lock-box. The same key operates the gate lock and the Casita lock. We change the combination after each guest for everyone's safety.

Your Lock-Box Combination: X - X - X - X

In the Casita, you will find a memory-foam queen bed made with fresh sheets. There will be fresh towels and washcloths in the bathroom, so no need to pack those. The kitchenette will be stocked with a few breakfast items, such as cereal and fresh muffins, milk and orange juice in the fridge, and a selection of Keurig coffees and creamers. A bottle of red wine will also be there for your enjoyment, should you desire.

We have free WiFi in the Casita. The login information is in the welcome packet, which you'll find next to the TV. The remote control for the TV is inside the nightstand.

Looking forward to your upcoming visit. Feel free to reach out any time.

Ben

One of the 9 steps in turning the Casita is to place the lockbox with the updated combination on the gate. The key inside the lockbox opens both the gate at the street as well as the Casita itself.

<u>About the Locks</u>

When we took possession of our house after closing, we received a box full of keys. There were locks by different manufacturers in every door. This kind of thing really drives me mad, and yet it happens each time I buy a new building.

I tossed all of the keys and changed out all of the locks to one manufacturer. This enabled me to key all of the doors to a master key but also to key the front gate and the Casita to another key. So, the key that I put into the lockbox for guests opens only the gate and the Casita, while the master key opens those plus every other lock in the house.

The lockbox I use is one of those simple combination boxes from Home Depot. I've never had any issues with guests being unable to access the key. The system works very well for us.

Conclusion

Managing the guests, specifically as it relates turning the unit, is likely the biggest deterrent for lots of people. I am here to tell you not to worry. This can be very easy!

It is important to understand, however, that just as with everything else in real estate investing, the ease or difficulty of turns is teed-up by the house hack that you've bought. If you buy the wrong kind of asset, everything is more difficult. The maintenance is more difficult. The marketing is more difficult. And the turns are more difficult.

So the key, for you, is to buy the right thing. If you follow the precepts laid out in this book, you should find much success!

Epilogue

I discovered a while back that all I have to do in order to achieve personal and professional success is help people. In fact, the more people I help, the more abundance comes into my life.

As I go through this life as an incorrigible entrepreneur willing to try anything once, I am aware that the most help I can offer is to both share with you my failures in hopes of helping you avoid the same mistakes and to share my successes in hopes of shortening your learning curve so as to enable your success faster.

This book is another such installment of Ben's helpful strategies. I wrote it, because having stumbled on the technique of house hacking, it became clear to me that it is possibly the most viable and versatile strategy for many of you today.

First of all, house hacking is quite simply the ticket to locational freedom. In my own life, this Casita house hack has facilitated a tremendous upgrade in our lifestyle while decreasing our cost of living. And now that I am aware, I plan on using the principles outlined in this book forever. The next stop may be Hawaii or a beach house in the Caribbean. And yes, while the cost of a house there may be 4 times as much, the house-hacking possibilities are 10 times as abundant.

Another use for this strategy can be to simply underwrite the cost of living for those of you living in high-priced markets, including the coastal markets in the US. Hopefully, my friend Peggy finds some of the ideas herein useful.

Additionally, house hacking is quite simply the single most achievable and most easily executed strategy for those who want to enter the game of real estate investing. As I outlined in the book, everything from the down-payment requirements to financing terms to management is so much easier with house hacking.

Indeed, this technique is one of those few tools in the belt which can facilitate a lot of different solutions to a lot of different problems for a lot of different people. This is why I published this book!

I hope you enjoyed reading this book. Thank you indeed for picking it up. I hope this book helps you to find and execute your own house hack.

Good Luck to you in this endeavor!

Ben

Next Steps

Okay! This is where you take action, and these are the steps I can recommend.

Step 1: Download Additional Materials

Throughout this book, I mentioned additional items that I created for you. Some of these will help you internalize the concepts. Others are there to simply jump-start the processes involved with house hacking. Included are the following:

The Book Guide This guide will help keep all of the main concepts fresh in your mind.

Understanding Market Values This eBook will detail the process of estimating market value on both SFR and Multifamily.

Casita Guest Handbook	The Handbook is an actual hard-copy printed folder that we leave in the Casita for our guests. Feel free to model yours in the same way, and be sure to add as much helpful information as necessary to help your guests enjoy their stay.
Guest Checkout List	This contains the checkout instructions.

You can find all of these documents ready for instant download on my website at:

www.JustAskBenWhy.com/househack

Step 2: Decide what you want!

The book you just finished reading is ultimately about one simple concept—freedom. House hacking is nothing more than just another tool to add to your arsenal. But, the tools are useless unless you know what you want—what you *really* want—out of life.

That said, the first thing you need to do is find a quiet place, close your eyes, and meditate on the question—*what do I want?* The images you see—this is what your nirvana looks like. Don't be afraid of it and don't feel stupid. Embrace it!

You learned in this book that you can have anything you want, so long as it makes money. Once you know what it is you want, the next step is to figure out how to make money with it. But for now, just figure out what you want. Among other things, figure out where you want to be!

Step 3: JustAskBenWhy.com

If what you want is in some way related to real estate investing, I encourage you to visit my site for more specific information:

www.JustAskBenWhy.com

Step 4: Let's Connect

I am really hopeful that this book inspires you to do something bold! I am excited to offer support in any way I can. Let's connect!

www.FaceBook.com/JustAskBen

www.Twitter.com/JustAskBen

And, of course, feel free to shoot me an email any time:

ben@JustAskBenWhy.com

Step 5: Do it!!!

One Last Thing

Would you do me a huge favor, please, and buy someone you care about a copy of this book. The economics of the world are changing, and I believe so strongly that this house-hacking tool can be so helpful to so many. Help me spread the word, please.

And, finally, if you liked this book, would you leave a review here? The more reviews I get, the more people I can reach.

Thank you so much!

Made in the USA
Lexington, KY
30 July 2017